THE SUNDAY TIMES

Successful Project Management

Trevor L Young

KOGAN PAGE | *CREATING SUCCESS*

First Indian Edition 2002
Reprinted 2005

Kogan Page India Private Limited
4262/3 Ansari Road
Daryaganj
New Delhi 110 002.

ISBN 81-7554-188-1

Published by Vinod Vasishtha for Kogan Page India Private Limited,
4262/3 Ansari Road, Daryaganj, New Delhi - 110 002 and
printed & bound at Raj Press, R-3 Inderpuri, New Delhi - 110 012.

contents

introduction

Over the past 10 years, project management has become a topical subject of interest in all types of business. This renewed interest has generated many publications on the subject. So how can this book help you? The purpose is to explore the steps you can take to raise significantly the probability of success with your projects. The contents are, therefore, aimed at managers who are concerned about getting better results from projects in their organisations and project managers who have already found themselves by accident or design responsible for one or more projects.

This demands a starting point that is based on a simple but highly significant presumption – that you already have at least some experience of involvement in one or more projects. You may have considered your last project to end with a successful conclusion and you are now seeking ways to improve that success by degrees. Perhaps you are aware of the possibility of improving the degree of success to ensure the results are received with greater acclaim. Or you may have been less fortunate and involved in a project that has been labelled a failure by someone. It is a common experience that once a project is called anything less than a success by someone, the story becomes a legend even if it is not true. Perceptions of failure spread like electricity down the wire and everyone knows and will even decide why success was eluded. Regrettably the legend includes you as the primary owner of the perceived failure since you were the project manager.

how to use this book

Of course success in any venture is never guaranteed. The steps towards achieving success are vulnerable to many factors. Many are predictable and some are not so easy to predict. The objective is to help you with a practical approach to improve the way you start and conduct your next project to overcome some of the factors that impede success:

- Chapter 1 discusses the perceptions of success and how we define success with projects.
- Chapter 2 outlines the importance of creating an appropriate climate for success and the roles and responsibilities for this climate to generate success with all the projects.
- Chapter 3 identifies the project process phases and key steps for success.
- Chapters 4 and 5 concentrates on the initial conception and definition phases of the project.
- Chapter 6 specifically looks at how to manage the stakeholders, a key step for success.
- Chapter 7 discusses how to manage risks in the project, another significant key step for success.
- Chapters 8–10 concentrate on the planning, execution and closure phases of the project.

checklists and watchpoints

Throughout the text you will find short checklists to give guidance. Use these as starting points and add your own appropriate questions. Also you will find watchpoints, specific guide notes that are important for your attention in your drive to achieve success with your project.

To adopt the processes given here may require you to change the way you work and set aside some of those practices that have become habits for you. Changing your habits is never easy to accept as a necessity, particularly as you believe your working practices have served you well up to now. Such a conflict makes you feel uncomfortable because you are entering an area of low experience. All the processes and techniques discussed in this book are proven, practical ways to help you. It will be to your advantage to learn them and find a way to apply them in your situation.

Everything discussed here can be applied to any type of project irrespective of the nature of your business and regardless of whether your customer is internal or external to your organisation. Finally you will find some additional reading when project work has really attracted your attention for future development.

1

what is success?

When a major project is perceived as a failure, someone will take up the challenge the organisation faces to avoid a repeat. This evaluation may be prompted by a new product or service being late to market, customer needs not being satisfied or even a realization that a large sum of money has been expended with little or no chance of any return on the investment made. The result could be a question of organizational survival in a highly competitive market environment if there are a succession of failures. The initial focus of the evaluation in such situations is nearly always the degree to which project management skills were understood and employed during the project time span. Then it is often seen that the project manager and the team have done all the right things at the right time within the project.

Yet something clearly went wrong somewhere and a wider view is taken to identify cause. Then it becomes more obvious that project management competencies and skills alone are no guarantee of success. Many parts of any organization have a strong influence on every project initiated and an understanding of project management and the processes used must be part of everyone's learning today in all departments, not just the project team.

what happens to the project?

Someone identifies an opportunity for some new business, somewhere in the organisation. A project team is assembled and a project manager assigned. The team may be assembled with individuals from all or just one or two of these departments. The Management Information System is designed to help run the business, not projects, yet this opportunity may be perceived by a few people as a vital element of future survival for the business. The project is conducted in a virtual envelope and when it looks as if it might have a 'successful outcome', the Manufacturing department is informed. Then it is discovered that the project team made some wrong assumptions and capital expenditure is required. Perhaps forward manufacturing plans to meet the order book have no capacity to run tests and pilot samples for at least six months. Sales department get wind of what is happening and start shouting for the new product and major conflicts arise as every department highlights its own needs, to avoid making changes now and accommodate the project team. The consequence is demotivation of the project team, as no one appears to have clear responsibility for getting decisions made to promote the outputs from the project team.

How often does this type of situation develop with projects? This is a constant risk associated with project work if the projects in an organisation are treated as something separate and disconnected with the normal day-to-day operations of the business.

How can this be corrected in the real world? The climate in which the projects are conducted has to be created with the active involvement of all the departments, some of which may initially think they have no part to play in the project. There are few projects in any organisation today that do not involve, influence or affect many or all departments. Managers of these departments and the senior management of the organisation cannot afford to risk ignoring the project activities that they consider do not affect them. They may not initially see any linkage between their activities and the project, or consider the project is a waste of valuable money and resource effort. Or the project may become the pawn in a political game as managers individually express open support, cynicism or opposition to the project to fit their own personal agendas.

defining success

Success is one of those words that conjure up a picture we paint in our minds. What sort of picture do you see for success? Is it huge financial gain, public recognition, promotion to senior management or just a great personal internalised feeling of achieving something you had initially determined was something to attain? Some of us find it easier and are more naturally able to paint that picture than others, and we respect and admire the 'true visionary' who can turn that picture into words like Martin Luther King or Nelson Mandela.

your view of success

exercise

Think about the projects you have either led as a project manager, in which you have been a team member or even those where you have been merely an uninvolved observer. Now try to put into words how you would describe a successful project: 'My idea of a successful project is characterised by...'

comments

If we look in the dictionary for a definition of success we find it defined as 'attainment of object, or of wealth, fame or position' with synonyms such as victory, accomplishment, achievement, prosperity, attainment, fruition, winning. In a project environment this raises some questions:

- Do any of these words appear in your description of the picture you have painted above?
- For all those projects where you have some direct experience, how many fit your description?
- Does the word 'customer' appear in your description of success?
- Does your description include some measurement of benefit?

Now ask some of your colleagues if their view is the same. Explore how their perception of success varies from your view. You will agree on some characteristics and differ on others because perceptions of success are driven by individual beliefs about what was expected as the outcomes from any project. If these expectations are not satisfied then the project is labelled as only a partial success. A partial success often becomes perceived as a failure just because some of these expectations were not satisfied. Ask some senior managers for their views on the same projects and discover if there is any variance with your view.

success depends on who is measuring

Clearly the perception of success is dependent on who has established some metrics and is then making the measurements. Most projects traditionally have some common elements:

- ***The customer*** – the 'purchaser' of the project outcomes or results. This individual may be internal or external to the organisation and represent the 'end users' of these outcomes. The customer may be viewed as the individual who demanded the project initially or became engaged or involved after the project was completed. There may be several customers with different needs leading to a range of requirements for the project.
- ***The sponsor*** – the individual inside the organisation who has accountability for the project. The sponsor drives the project in the right direction to benefit the organisation.
- ***The project manager*** – the individual who has the day to day responsibility for the project work and is charged with completing this work on time, to an agreed budgeted cost and quality.
- ***The project team*** – the people who carry out all the tasks planned in the project schedule.
- ***The resource managers*** – the departmental managers who have direct responsibility for the people you seek to engage in your project team to complete the project work. These team members may be part-time on your project, work on other projects concurrently or be dedicated full time to your project for a fixed time period.

Each of these individuals separately or collectively in groups have different reasons for qualifying and defining success. Conversely they can usually very quickly give you an opinion on failure or advise you what will lead to failure. Just how each can contribute to success or failure is key to your management of the project. As we examine each of the key steps to achieving success we will take a look at the actions you can take to avoid failure and enable a successful outcome.

what are the perceived causes of failure?

Many reasons are quoted for projects failing in organisations. Some of the more common reasons quoted, often in combination are given as:

- Poor definition of objectives at the outset.
- Inability to build a truly cross functional team.
- Lack of understanding of team member availability and capacity to do the work.
- Inadequate schedule management leading to schedule creep – elastic schedules.
- Weak leadership.
- Lack of senior management commitment.
- Minimising complexity with consequent technical problems not resolved.
- Inability to anticipate problems.
- Poor planning and control – the feeling that planning is an unnatural act.
- Too many uncontrolled changes with consequent scope creep.
- Resistance to change.
- Inadequate resources.
- No effective communication process.
- Assumed knowledge, skills and experience of team members.
- Scope not clear or controlled as project progresses.
- Confused roles and responsibilities – who does what when?
- 'I'll do it my way' (Great song because my part's okay, but lousy management).
- Titanic Complex – 'This project is sponsored by the MD and is unsinkable' so no one is looking for icebergs!
- Speed is only for Formula One racing junkies – we'll take as long as it takes.

- Over-optimism about time due to our innate ability to underestimate everything.
- All projects here are runaway trains – once started they just keep on going.
- We've done enough. Let's declare victory and go home.
- We didn't even have to involve the customers – we just told them after we finished.
- Success criteria? What are they?

reduce the probability of failure

The watch for potential failure is a continuous activity that must be a responsibility of everyone involved not just the project manager. Risk management processes are an essential and integral part of project management and will help reduce the probability of failure. Creating the platinum version of the product or service is ambitious and often more complex. Of course the team are having fun, justifying their existence and sustaining their continued employment!

It is easy for the team to convince themselves that providing a feature rich product or service is obviously going to be seen by the customers as more beneficial eventually. In reality you continue to do this development with a high risk that a competitor will take the business well before your organisation, reducing your potential market share. Grabbing a competitor's market share is never an easy path to follow. The reduction of the probability of failure must, therefore, take a wider view than just the internal activities of the team and their project work.

watchpoint

Use the reasons for project failure as a list of things to avoid and create a checklist of actions you can take to turn potential failure into a high probability of success.

2

the climate for success

In every organisation today there is always a list of systems, processes, services and products that need to be improved, modified or even introduced to make the business more secure and grow. Over the past decades businesses in all sectors have seen many techniques offered to help them achieve these changes to improve performance. Unfortunately the enduring benefits these initiatives promised have not always been successful in sustaining and growing the business.

In fact in many organisations the merest mention of the word 'initiative' creates an immediate adverse reaction in the staff: 'Not another one!' Senior management has frequently failed to recognise that their role does not end when the initiative is framed, written down and published. They will even commit huge sums of money to provide training and internal publicity and then believe that it will then just happen. Worse still, the senior management believe that because they have endorsed the initiative it is happening when in reality it has gone sadly wrong. When challenged they are unable to explain why the benefits did not accrue and will use excuses like: 'It was the wrong time to do something like that in this organisation.' The cost may run into millions every year and even result in closure and release of a complete workforce.

why do initiatives appear to fail?

Some should never have started but are driven by what is fashionable in the prevailing business environment. Some are introduced by whim alone and no real study of the need and real analysis of the expected outcomes and benefits. A large number fail to have any real impact because the organisation has no discipline in following processes demanded by the initiative or the new processes conflict with processes that some parts of the organisation have had embedded for several years. This suggests the organisation does not understand how to introduce and control changes and has not matured a 'global' approach to managing change. Even worse is the possibility that the organisation has no shared clarity of strategy that drives decision making processes.

some definitions

Most of these initiatives have a number of common elements that impact the organisation. They provide:

- a unique opportunity to learn and acquire new skills and knowledge;
- a way to improve performance of everyone involved [in the organisation];
- an opportunity to create new and more effective working practices and habits;
- a high profile way to initiate major new developments of products or services.

These elements are consistent with the characteristics of a project and more broadly consistent with project management concepts. Before taking this further let us introduce some important definitions:

> **definition**
>
> ***A project*** is a temporary endeavour to achieve some specific objectives in a defined time.

Projects may vary considerably in size and duration, involving a small group of people or large numbers in different parts of the organisation, even working in different countries. It is usually unique in content and unlikely to be repeated again in exactly the same way.

> **definition**
>
> ***Project management*** is a dynamic process that utilises the appropriate resources of the organisation in a controlled and structured manner to achieve some clearly defined objectives identified as strategic needs. It is always conducted within a defined set of constraints.

The way forward now being adopted by many organisations is to use ***project management*** to manage change. Since projects are about change – creating something or a state we need but do not have, then it seems the natural management process to adopt.

In many situations we see the need for more than one project to achieve the final outcome desired. It is often convenient to divide the work involved into a collection or 'suite' of projects across an organisation, particularly where different national cultures may have an influence or functional requirements make implementation relatively easier to accomplish. Additionally some projects in the suite may take longer than others and spread over more than one fiscal year. For these and numerous other reasons we introduce the concept of Programmes.

> **definition**
>
> ***A Programme*** is a collection of inter-dependent projects, managed in a coordinated manner that together will provide the desired outcomes. Programmes are usually phased, with target end dates of the initial phases well defined and committed. Subsequent phases are defined as the initial phase approaches completion, enabling new related projects to be initiated.

If there is more than one project involved or several related together with phasing over a period of time then we use ***programme management*** to manage and control the change process.

> **definition**
>
> ***Programme management*** is the utilisation of project management and its inherent processes to manage a collection of closely inter-dependent projects in a controlled and structured manner to achieve some clearly defined objectives identified as strategic needs.

The processes employed for programmes and projects are similar. Neither addresses the key issue of what the organisation is striving to achieve in strategic terms. To solve this issue we need to introduce the concept of ***portfolio management*** to relate the initiatives to the organisation strategy.

definition

Portfolio management is concerned with managing all active programmes and projects along with future opportunities to ensure the resources of the organisation are deployed in the most effective manner to achieve strategic objectives.

Portfolio management is an important process in seeking success with all our programmes and projects. This is not intended to suggest that programmes or projects are only the company-wide initiatives. The majority of such activities are much more focused on supporting the development and growth of the business with new services, products or systems to serve the market place. All of these represent a change from the prevailing situation and are identified as a need for business growth.

Generally we will address projects in this book although much of the content applies equally to programmes, since these are really just much larger projects with some additional characteristics.

projects – are they just an accident?

Project management has been called the 'accidental profession'. One of the most common ways to drop into the role is to identify a significant problem or business opportunity and then be told to pull a project team together to deal with the problem or opportunity. You then find that this is really a way of keeping you well overloaded with work. If you are successful you hand the manager who gave you the role initially an opportunity of demonstrating their ability to predict business or customer needs and gain kudos for their forward vision and justify their position. If the 'project' fails the consequence is never mentioned again and life in your department continues as before. The project is managed as a departmental activity hidden from any organisational visibility.

a common misconception

The idea for the project will almost certainly be created from your knowledge and experience of the organisation, customer base or market place. This 'technical' knowledge is often considered as the perfect qualification for leading a project team to a successful outcome. You are the 'technical expert' and any subsequent success or failure is attached to you. It is also commonly believed that as the expert you can manage the work of the project in the same way as normal day to day activities and will take the same amount of time. These misconceptions create a situation where false assumptions are made and creating false expectations of cost and time to complete that can rarely be satisfied.

what's the current climate?

The projects are conducted within the prevailing climate in your organisation. Perhaps this climate is:

- stormy and riddled with conflict;
- continually subject to reactive activities due to systems failures;
- subject to outside influences not identified as possible happenings;

- focused totally on today and never considering tomorrow.

If this is the case, then for much of the time the organisation will strive to overcome the conditions that prevail in which everyone tries to get their job done to the best of their ability. People are left operating in a climate of many unknowns, trying to resolve conflicts with no analysis of the future, no risk analysis and no forecast of what problems will hit them tomorrow. Senior managers are continually reacting and fire-fighting, not looking ahead to business development. Project work comes to a halt as team members are continually re-assigned or overloaded with operational and fire-fighting activities. The climate for project work to succeed does not exist in such a culture.

It is essential for senior managers to create and work continually to sustain the climate for success. As project manager you are more likely to be remembered for your failures rather than your successes so you have a key role to play in supporting and maintaining the climate for success.

what influences the climate?

The climate in an organisation at any time is influenced by several integrated elements including:

- the organisational culture;
- the organisational structure;
- the business strategy;
- the infrastructure for projects.

Each has a significant impact on whether the climate is appropriate for project success.

the organisational culture

The prevailing culture of an organisation is often quoted as the reason why things do not happen as planned or intended. The concept of culture is difficult to define or explain precisely and little consensus exists on its meaning or relationship with the climate in the organisation.

A common and simple way of defining culture is 'how things get done round here'. It generally identifies what is 'acceptable and not acceptable' and what behaviours are encouraged and discouraged. Most attempts to open this definition to analysis focus on:

> the collection of traditions, values, policies, beliefs and attitudes that constitute a pervasive context for everything we do in an organisation.

So we can expect culture to be influenced by the system of rites, rituals, patterns of communication and expected behaviours that are acceptable.

Management has a significant influence on culture through their style of leadership and the staff acceptance of the climate created. This affects the environment in which the organisation operates with a quick response and adaptation to change when it is required.

the organisation structure

Many organisations are still structured formally into a hierarchy. This is easy to comprehend and manage and creates a (relatively) straightforward management structure that allows career progression, delegation of authority and clear demarcation of responsibilities based on skills and function. This type of structure has evolved as 'best practice' and supports a product or service-oriented organisation where each function has a part to play that is well defined.

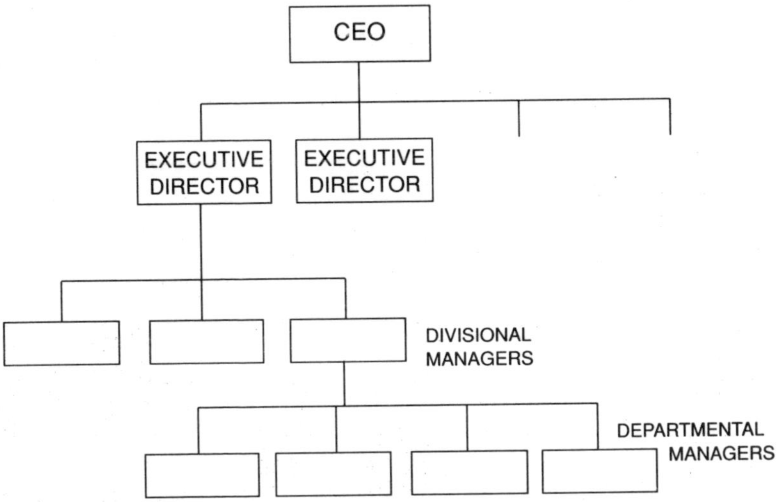

Figure 2.1 *A hierarchical structure*

Introduce the project into this structure and difficulties immediately appear. If a change of activity or project is confined to one vertical leg or functional area there is generally no difficulties beyond managing resource availability and controlling time management. As soon as a project team is required that demands resources to be pulled out of this vertical oriented functional structure problems occur that demonstrate the structure is more than a collection of formal organisation charts. Structure includes all the systems and sub-systems in the organisation:

- reporting relationships – the true power structure;
- communication channels – formal and informal;
- decision making processes;
- accountability;
- reward systems – compensation, benefits and motivational;
- acceptable norms and practices.

When functions are duplicated in the individual parts of the formal hierarchy as we frequently observe for budget accountability reasons, the systems become even more complex.

Projects can and do succeed 'in spite of the organisation structure' when the project leader is strongly committed to break down the numerous barriers between the business groups that are continually getting in the way. This takes considerable effort that could be better expended on the project work.

> **watchpoint**
>
> Collaborative working across the whole structure is a key to project success, as is recognition that assigning an individual to a project team is a dedicated assignment for the whole project.

This creates a weak matrix structure (shown in Figure 2.2) for projects that has some formality and acceptance by the management. It introduces the need for new systems of performance management and financial control but with care these can be managed.

the business strategy

It is important to understand clearly why any project is initiated and establish a defined process to focus on the reasons and purpose. The link here is the business strategy of the organisation.

Although the vision of the senior management team is not always obvious or clearly stated, there is always a fundamental direction that the business is striving to sustain. This drives the strategy that normally can be simplified down to three elements:

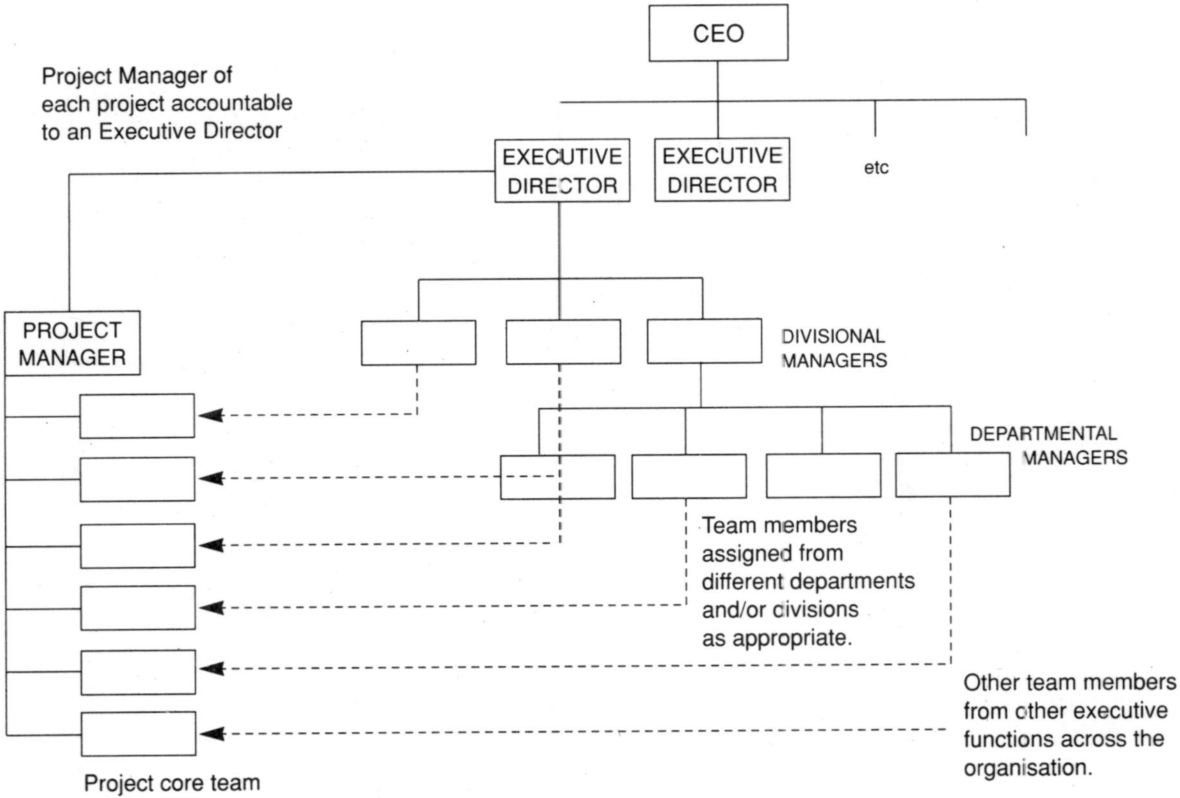

Figure 2.2 *A project-based matrix structure*

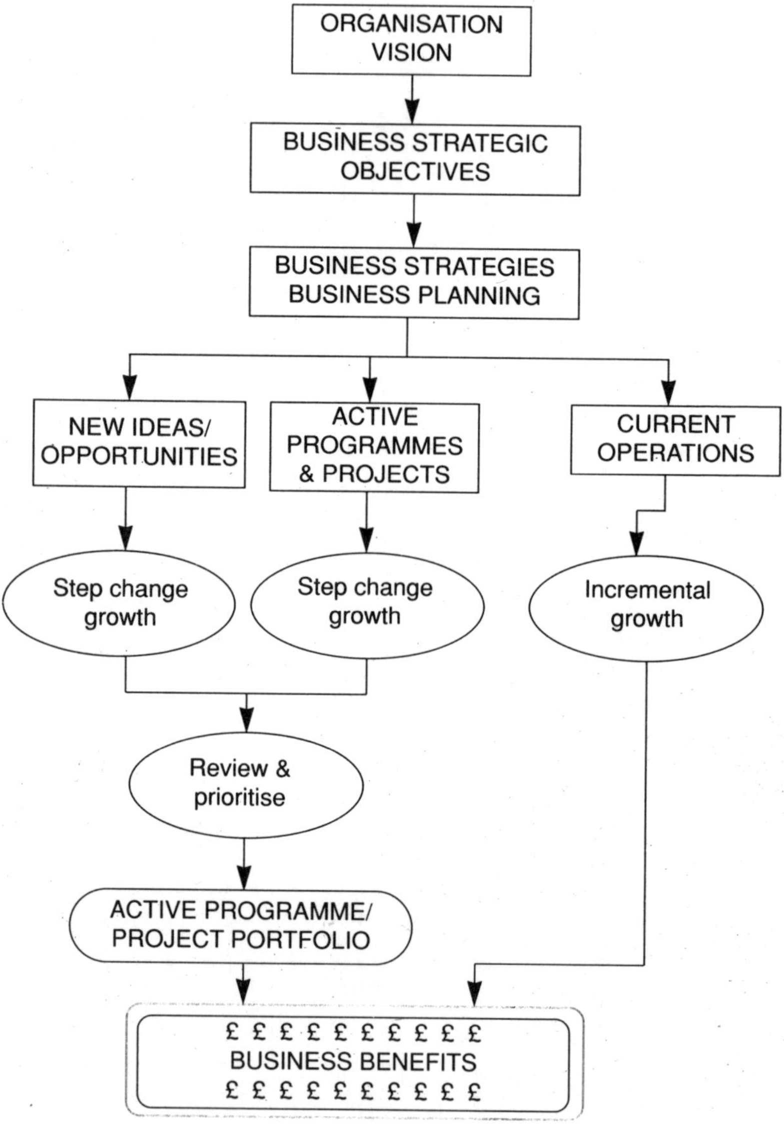

Figure 2.3 *How strategy and projects are related*

- sustaining existing activities for incremental growth and benefit creation;
- maintaining a focus on initiated projects to gain additional benefits;
- identifying new projects that will provide further additional benefits.

If projects are undertaken that do not align with the business strategy then there is a risk that valuable resources and funds are being used to create something the business does not need. Additionally, there is a hidden lost opportunity cost because those resources and funds are not being applied to something the business does need.

Programme management is the basis of managing the complete portfolio. The concept of programme in this context is a collection of related projects that work together to provide benefits over a period of time. This does not preclude the use of independent projects that also form part of the total portfolio. Generally, programme management is concerned with overall strategic objectives and is very suited to enabling the management of the impact and benefits from a number of projects.

Clearly the essential starting point is the business strategy. Any new programme or project should not be initiated without first testing that it fits the existing strategy or justifies in special circumstances, a change to the strategy. If the proposed programme or project does not fit and support the strategy the question must be asked – 'Why are we attempting to do this?' It is remarkable how managers will justify the strategic fit by clever use of semantics, particularly as strategies are frequently fairly broad statements in their own right. Strategic fit alone does not guarantee success, it merely serves to ensure we are doing the right thing and not doing something that has no alignment to business needs.

the organisation infrastructure

Although culture, formal structure, and business strategy provide important contributions towards the prevailing climate, the cement that holds everything together is the operating infrastructure. This is what enables good decisions to be made and ensure focus for all the activities and projects is directed towards satisfying the needs and objectives of the business strategy.

Creating this infrastructure ensures all the key players in the organisation project environment have clearly defined roles and responsibilities. A balanced, holistic view of the business must be taken to ensure all the resources available are effectively utilised to grow and develop the business. This transcends the more parochial view often supported by the hierarchical structure. Decisions can only be effective if they are based on real and accurate information. This creates the need for supporting systems to collect data to enable management to make informed decisions rather than rely on inspired guesswork. The selection and continuation of all project activities is costly, consuming resources, and must be based on informed decisions.

the operating climate for projects

The operating climate is constructed from many contributing elements from the culture, structure and strategy, but we can collect these into some key elements that make a significant difference to achieving success with all the projects:

alignment with business strategy

The right projects and programmes that support achieving the business strategy are selected or effort may be directed to producing results that are not needed or do not contribute to business growth. A carefully constructed business case is a significant piece of work to assist making this judgement.

effective decision making

Senior management based on informed judgement that is trusted, respected and supported across the organisation should make decisions on projects. Otherwise the decisions made in one part of the organisation may be in conflict with decisions made in other parts of the organisation. In some situations duplication of effort can occur or projects that should be suspended or cancelled are allowed to continue like 'runaway trains'.

resource management

Resource needs of existing commitments must be visible and the capacity to take on more work needs to be clear to everyone. If resource planning is not practised you do not know if you have sufficient resource capacity to complete what has already started let alone start new projects.

forward planning

The selection of projects requires the organisation to plan ahead using adequate intelligence information gathered from the market place and customers. No planning will lead to biased decisions with lack of focus on critical areas of potential business growth and lost opportunities.

financial management

Adequate funding must be available to provide every project with a budget. If you do not know what it will cost the business cannot adequately plan cash flow and make provisions for future project needs, which may lead to suspended or cancelled projects.

portfolio management

Timescale and completion targets need to be agreed to meet the business and/or customer needs and plan the redeployment of resources. Maintaining a list of active projects and those waiting to start is essential to inform everyone of priorities and relative importance of those on the list. Without this listing interdependencies are not clear and the authorised projects are not visible to the whole organisation.

roles and responsibilities

All the key players in the business must have a clear notion of their responsibilities with respect to both the normal operating activities and the projects agreed as part of the total portfolio. This avoids confusion and also clarifies where authority exists to make decisions and avoid unnecessary slippage and delays in projects.

defined roles and responsibilities – the key players

For your project to achieve a successful outcome you need to identify the principal roles and their responsibilities and how they will work together – the infrastructure. For every project, apart from the originator of the idea or opportunity we need:

- someone who needs the benefits – the company management;

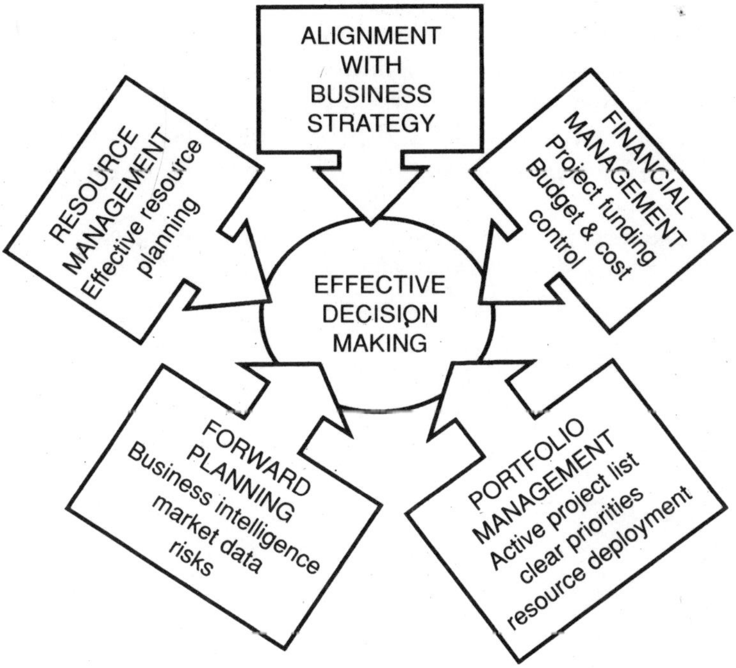

Figure 2.4 *The project climate for success – key elements*

- someone who wants to use the outcomes – the customer, a stakeholder;
- someone who is accountable for achieving the benefits – the sponsor;
- someone who is accountable for the project work – the project manager;
- someone who undertakes the project work – the project team;
- someone who provides the resources – line managers;
- we also acquire: others who are interested, affected by or want to influence the outcomes – the stakeholders.

Together this whole group creates an infrastructure, and their behaviour collectively can determine the degree of success that is achievable with all the projects. The linkage and relationships are shown in Figure 2.5.

This forms a clearly defined project organisation infrastructure that is overlaid on the functional hierarchy to establish:

> ... a clear definition of ownership at each level in the organisation with clearly defined roles and responsibilities.

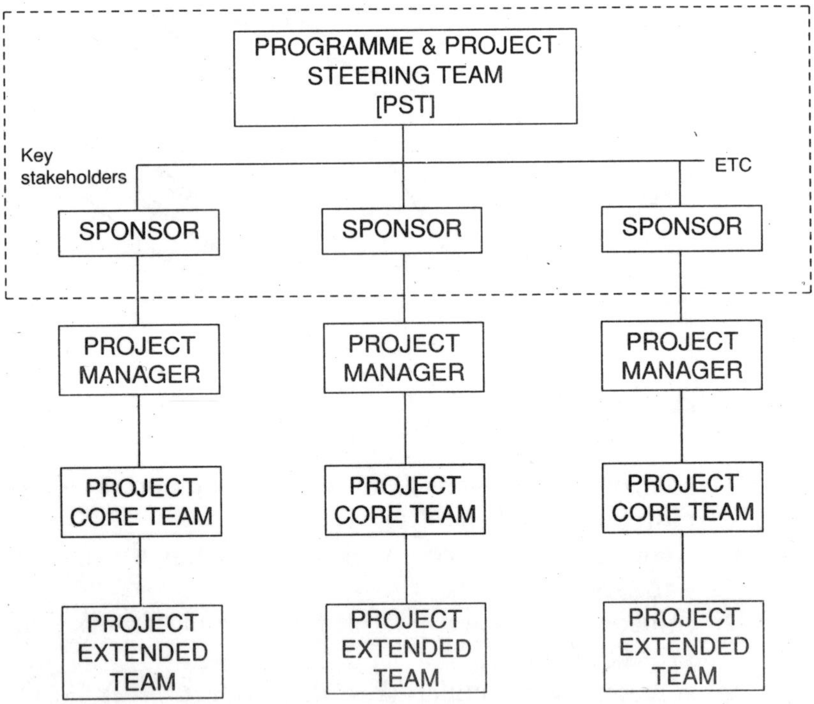

Figure 2.5 *The infrastructure for projects*

programme steering team

This group made up of senior managers, who are the ***project sponsors***, meets at regular intervals to review the status of all active projects. They select and initiate new projects, resolve major issues and decide the prioritisation of project activity in the organisation. Responsibilities include:

- management of the total portfolio of projects;
- ensuring projects are aligned to business strategy and objectives;
- giving strategic direction;
- maintaining focus on customer and business needs;
- ensuring environmental influences are taken into account [internal and external];
- prioritising all active projects and their resourcing;
- resolving escalated issues related to cross-functional working;
- ultimate decision forum for all major problems and issues;
- approves start-up, suspend and abort decisions of projects.

The *programme steering team* (PST) is essential for projects that cross functional boundaries to ensure decisions are made collaboratively and carried out effectively. Unfortunately at senior management level in many organisations today, teamwork is not always regarded as important. This leaves the PST ineffective because it appears to have a low added value to the projects that are active. This is frequently because the Sponsors do not accept their role or responsibilities.

project sponsor

The project sponsor for any project, usually a senior manager, is accountable (to the PST) for the overall performance of their projects to provide the organisation with the benefits promised in the approved business case. The sponsor must demonstrate to everyone involved a concern for success. Responsibilities include:

- ensuring project objectives are always aligned to business needs;
- selecting the project manager;
- approving the project definition;
- sustaining the project direction;
- ensuring priorities are maintained for all their projects;
- oversight of the project process and procedures, budget and control;
- reacting promptly to issues escalated to them for decisions;
- maintaining support and commitment;
- approving project plans, changes and status reports.

Since this is a role with accountability, it cannot be divided up and there should only be one sponsor for each project. The role should not be confused with a line management role; the sponsor does not own all the resources, but must commit to giving adequate time to these responsibilities.

the project manager

The *project manager* is accountable to the sponsor for the day to day management of the project work from the initial kick-off through to closure. Responsibilities include:

- selecting the core team with the project sponsor;
- identifying and managing the project stakeholders;
- defining the project and securing stakeholder approval;
- planning the project and securing stakeholder approval;

- identifying and managing the risks;
- securing resource commitments and allocating resources to the work;
- monitoring and tracking project progress;
- solving the problems that interfere with progress;
- controlling costs;
- leading the project team;
- informing stakeholders of progress status;
- delivering the project deliverables and benefits;
- managing performance of everyone involved with the project.

A new term has appeared in this chapter – the ***stakeholders***. These are the people who have a specific and clearly definable interest in your project – a stake in gambling terms! They are an important group of people and Chapter 6 is devoted to the management of this group.

the project team

The team members are responsible for the timely completion of all the work set out in the plan and schedule. Any individual team member may be accountable for a package of the work when delegated authority by the project manager, for example, as leader of a sub-project team.

There are two types of team member:

- *the core team member* – who remains part of the team right through the project and is often, or preferably, dedicated to the role full time or for a significant part of their capacity (more than 60 per cent).
- *the extended team member* – who joins the team for a limited period of time just when their skills and knowledge are needed and may have no further involvement

later in the project. Extended team members usually, but not always, work under the close direction of a core team member.

Responsibilities of the core team member include:

- to accept and commit to the team role;
- to liaise and work with other team members to get their work done;
- to contribute to the project documentation;
- to participate in planning and risk management;
- to monitor and manage progress of their assigned work packages;
- to resolve issues or escalate them to the project manager;
- to participate in problem solving;
- to identify potential risks, issues, opportunities;
- to support and assist other team members when appropriate.

Similar responsibilities exist for the extended team members and it is important for you to ensure that all team members accept these responsibilities from the outset. All team members must know to whom they report and in large complex projects this is often a source of confusion. If it helps, provide an organisation chart for the project and clearly define any authority you delegate to a core team member.

influence of organisational culture

Behaviour is strongly influenced by the perceptions people have of the internal climate. Acceptance or otherwise of the existing culture has a significant impact on climate. The key elements in the climate that impact on your ability to achieve success with your project also include some less obvious cultural influences:

- morale;
- mutual trust, support and respect for decisions;
- openness and integrity – avoiding confrontation;
- risk taking and optimism – recognition of risks and sharing in success;
- freedom of action – through accountability, pride and participation in decision making;
- commitment – a sense of belonging, avoiding confusion with clear responsibilities;
- collaboration – shared beliefs, teamwork and mutual assistance, minimising stress;
- training – opportunities to learn both on and off the job.

Paying specific attention to these influences is important for you. It is not enough to blame the management if the climate is going wrong. Perceptions of the climate are always stronger in the staff than among the management. This is not to suggest you are the standard-bearer for the whole organisation, but you can work with your team to ensure each influence is given adequate attention.

watchpoint

You must create the appropriate climate to enable you and your team to achieve success in your project. It is perhaps valid to note that all these influences are also considered as key to effective leadership, which indicates how closely climate and leadership are related.

3

the project process – key steps for success

One of the major contributors to success in all projects is for everyone involved to accept the discipline of using a common set of processes and procedures. This makes the sharing of information considerably easier, particularly when working across different sites and countries. Ideally this should extend also to using common computer software for data recording and scheduling. The combined result is the creation of a common, shared 'language' in the team that saves much time with the improved communication this brings.

watchpoint

Start your project by requiring everyone involved to conform to common processes and procedures and use standard documentation formats.

the project phases

The fundamental process for all projects is well established and proven. The process can be broken down into a number of definable phases with decision gates between each of the phases:

- project conception;
- project definition;
- project planning;
- project launch and execution;
- project closure;
- post-project evaluation.

Using this approach ensures all projects follow the same rational process and it is easy to review and report progress for each relative to the others. These phases are intentionally sequential and in each phase you will carry out specific activities that generate the data for decision processing. These activities are often referred to as 'key stages' as they may comprise several actual tasks carried out by more than one person.

Although each phase is treated as discrete with specific work to be completed, this does not signify they are 'one-off' activities. In reality the phases are often revisited during a project. Once a project is initiated, the need to reiterate some or all of the work done in the definition or planning phases is always a possibility as the project moves ahead in the execution phase. This is the nature of all projects since we are in a change process with many unknowns.

the phase gates

Introducing the phase gates into the project process ensures that decisions are confronted at the appropriate time in the project life cycle. The purpose is to ensure all the work in a phase is completed to the satisfaction of the customer and the programme steering team (PST). Some form of review and status report evidences this. The next phase cannot start without the gate being opened by the PST. This ensures that unnecessary effort is not expended before a 'continue' decision is made.

The phase gate serves to allow the PST to:

- validate the project is still needed;
- confirm the project risks are still acceptable;
- confirm the priority relative to other projects;
- accept any validation of the business case;
- make a 'GO/NO GO' decision about continuing.

Then three essential questions have to be asked:

- Is the project viable?
- Is the priority the same relative to other projects?
- Is the funding still available?

the phase gate – a constraint?

Does the concept of the gate at the end of the phase constitute a constraint by preventing some work in the next phase starting in the interests of saving time? The purpose of the gate is to focus everyone in taking a deep breath and just asking 'where are we now?' By regarding the PST decision as one to open the gate then entry is granted to the next phase. The PST can make this decision under specific circumstances even if the work of the previous phase is incomplete. The PST will expect to be given some clear plan to complete the work of a phase when opening the gate to the next phase in this way.

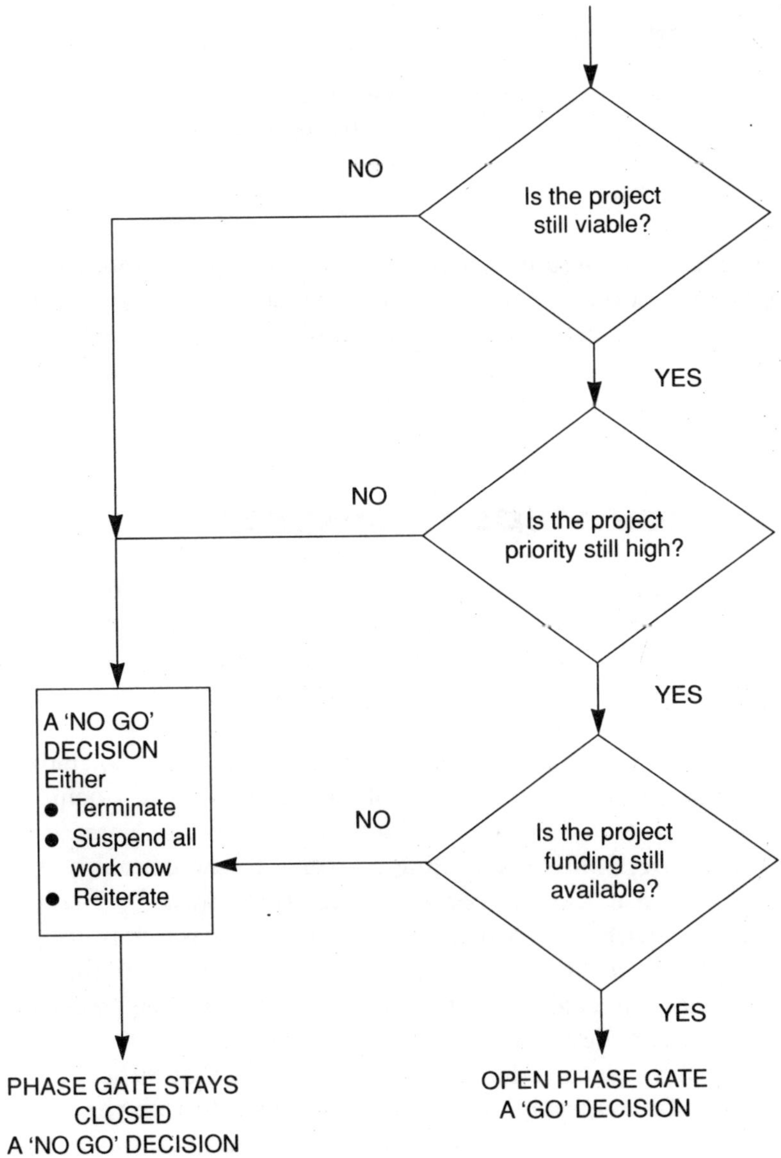

Figure 3.1 *The three key questions at each phase gate*

watchpoint

The phase gate should not be viewed as a constraint on the work of the project, but the gates should be regarded as mandatory for all projects.

Under certain circumstances the PST may require more work to be done in a phase before opening the gate, requesting a reiteration of some activities in more detail perhaps. Alternatively a decision may be made to suspend all work at the time to allow a more important project to take precedence.

the key steps to success

Each of the phases in a project is a key step towards a successful outcome. They are inter-dependent and all closely linked together in a logical manner. Two additional key steps, stakeholder management and risk management, have a significant impact on your success.

The business case is generated in the initial phase to enable a decision to proceed. This should remain a living document, subject to review and validation at each phase gate. If the project direction is proceeding contrary to the contents of the business case then a conscious decision must be made to continue with the project. The business case may require amendment itself, as new information becomes available. The impact of any changes to the business case must be assessed as part of the review and validation process.

You have to consider two other activities that impact on the project success, each having a continuous affect on the project performance. Risks are inherent in all projects and the management of risk is so important to your success it demands constant attention throughout the project. The effort may typi-

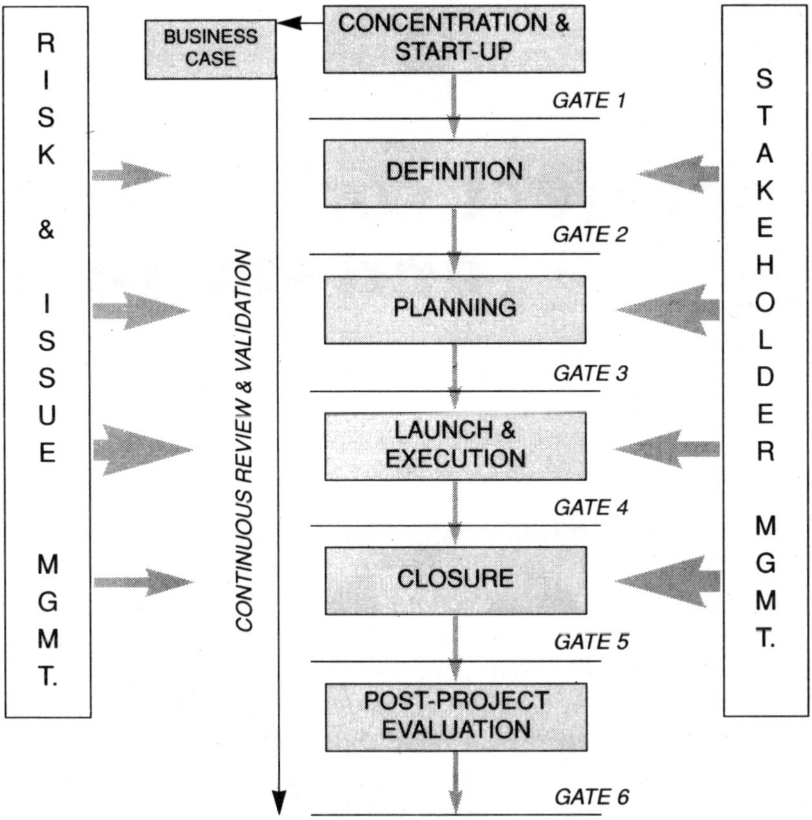

Figure 3.2 *The project phases, gates and key steps*

cally vary in each phase but risk management cannot be avoided if you seek to achieve a successful outcome. Similarly the management of your stakeholders is equally important. The stakeholders are often powerful sources of influence, and failure to manage them effectively can lead to disaster.

Each of the key steps, the phases of the project process, managing stakeholders and managing risk will be examined in more detail in the following chapters.

4

project conception and start-up

Most projects start from an initial idea, either from a potential customer or generated inside the organisation. Such ideas usually abound, far exceeding the available resources or funding for them all to be realistically turned into active projects. An initial screening process is essential if the organisation is not to over-commit resources and fail to deliver the desired results. This may involve some simple form of written proposal or just be a management decision to derive the initial business case. As a general rule it is preferable to derive the initial business case as a basis for informed decisions to be made.

selecting the right project

How often do organisations pour effort and money into a project to find at the end that no-one needs the outcome? There are two fundamental approaches to the selection process:

- a model generating quantitative data;
- and a model only generating qualitative data.

Selection is ultimately the decision of the senior management through the PST who need to be given enough data by you to make that decision. Selecting the wrong project may precipitate failure. If the climate described earlier is established then a strategic fit is a prerequisite for the PST to even consider a project proposal or business case. Every organisation should develop its own way of conducting this process to ensure the total portfolio of active projects does not demand more funds or resources than can be provided to achieve success.

Figure 4.1 illustrates one approach where the PST based on an initial business case or proposal conducts the initial screening of ideas and opportunities for projects. Those approved for more detailed scrutiny are then subject to a full needs and expectations analysis by an initial core team along with a review of resource needs. This data is used to generate a full business case for the proposed project. A secondary screening by the PST reviews the full business case before opening the gate to the definition phase. At each screening some opportunities are dropped completely or confined to a 'wait bin' for later consideration.

Any project selection process will induce the PST to ask some basic questions:

- Will the proposed project maximise profits?
- Will the proposed project:
  - maintain market share?
  - consolidate market position?
  - open up new markets?
- Will the project maximise utilisation of existing resources (ie people)?
- Will the project maximise the utilisation of existing manufacturing capacity?
- Will the project boost company image?
- Will the project increase risk faced by the company?
- Is the project scope within the company's current skills and experience?

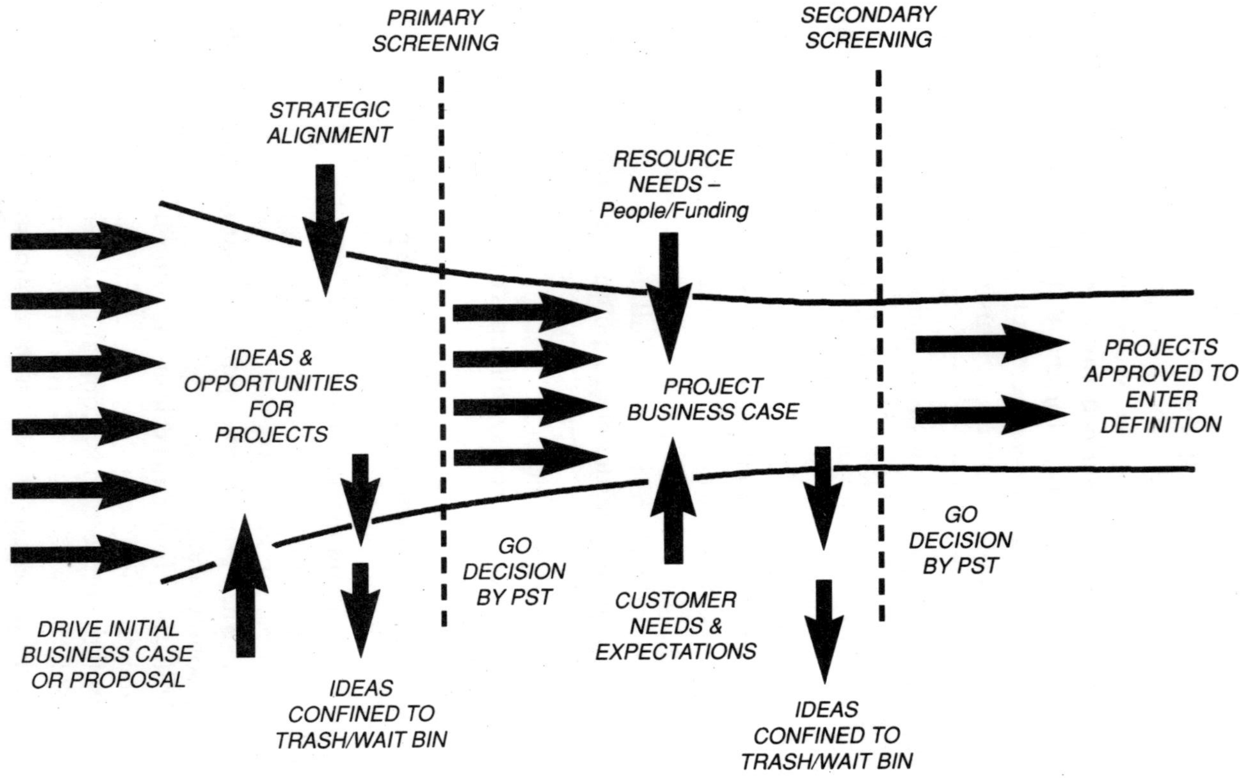

Figure 4.1 *Selecting the right projects*

The model can be constructed more rigorously by weighting some factors as more important than others indicating their value in contributing to the company objectives at the time. A detailed list of factors can be developed as appropriate based on:

- technology;
- marketing;
- finance;
- manufacture;
- personnel;
- administration.

This can lead to a long list of factors which is an advantage of this approach, and if these factors are then weighted a complex model can be derived that provides a score at the end. Such a model can readily be automated as a Web-based tool making it easy to apply sensitivity analysis to any of the factors.

quantitative models

Most quantitative models will focus on financial data to support the case. The data generated varies widely but may include information on:

- return on investment;
- return on net assets;
- breakeven and payback period;
- cost of risks;
- net present value and/or internal rate of return;
- cost/benefit analysis;
- sensitivity analysis;
- market data.

Each of the financial techniques has its merits and disadvantages so it is common to use more than one of the above. The more data generated, the more effort required later to re-validate and measure actual performance when all the focus is on the project work.

> **watchpoint**
>
> The business case is a key controlling document as the fundamental charter for the project and must be subject to regular revisiting, review and updating.

As more information becomes available through the project, complete and enhance the data in the business case. Do pay attention to your configuration management and record all revisions or additions made. It is important that the PST always refers to the latest revision when revisiting their decisions.

the start-up process

You are enthusiastic and keen to dive in and get going and show some activity. It is prudent to review just what information you can now assemble to ensure the project does not set off in the wrong direction. At this stage you should have clarified:

- who your sponsor is;
- who the customer and possible secondary customers are;
- who will use the results;
- the initial project core team – or likely candidates;
- other people who can influence the project – the stakeholders.

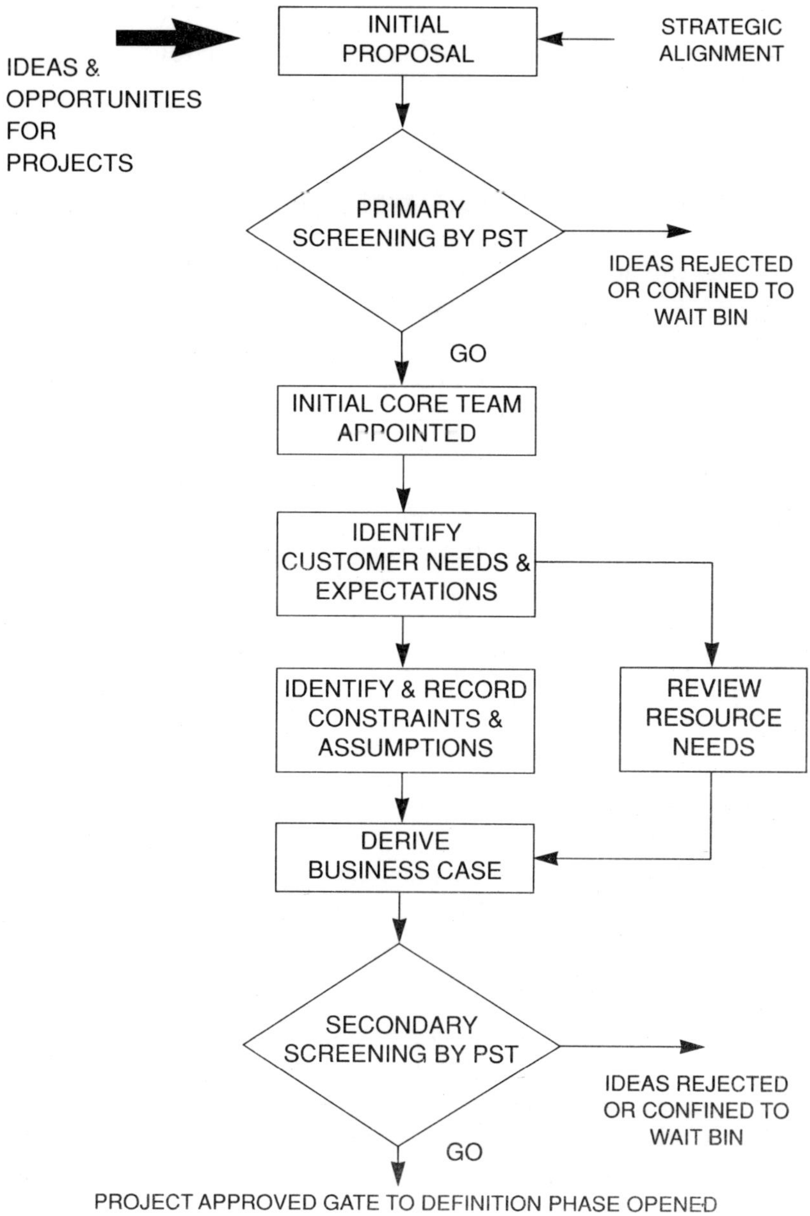

Figure 4.2 *The start-up process*

Your efforts and the work of the team will now be focused on gathering information from this group of individuals to kick-off the project.

customer needs and expectations

Defining the needs of the customer starts off a process that will ultimately allow you to produce deliverables specifically designed to meet the customer's expectations. Once you have established a clear understanding of the needs you can develop the requirements that drive the planning process.

Working with your customers can be frustrating. At times you will need to exercise all your communication skills to achieve a good, open relationship enabling the project to move ahead to achieve the agreed objectives. Deriving the needs statement is a product of a partnership between you and your customer. This places an obligation on your customer to enter into the partnership with a serious intent to contribute openly and not sit on hidden agendas.

watchpoint

Your business case will be permanently flawed if you do not understand the needs of your customer.

Exploring the needs of the customer will ultimately allow you to produce the list of deliverables specifically designed to meet the customer's expectations. Once you have established a clear understanding of the needs and validated these with the customer you can develop the requirements that drive the planning process.

Regard this as the preparation of the foundations of your project. Failure to give this activity appropriate time and effort will have continual impact on the project throughout its life.

You must make a particular effort to:

- understand the customer – explore priority and relative importance to other activities;
- understand the customer's environment in which they must operate;
- use political skills – not all customers are equal and some needs cannot be addressed;
- demonstrate your technical competence and awareness of their technical needs;
- convert ill-defined needs into practical solutions;
- keep an open mind and a creative approach;
- analyse the mixed signals you receive through personal influences on needs;
- attempt to expose the hidden expectations.

Your purpose at this stage is to turn the information you receive into a clear *statement of need* that you can reflect back to the customer for validation and acceptance with no ambiguity. Then both you and the customer are ready to collaborate fully to drive the project to a successful conclusion.

Avoid these potential traps:

1. Do not offer gold when silver is adequate – avoid striving for technical perfection beyond current capability or known state of the art. Simplicity is often more effective. Confirm that the customer understands the risks of going for leading edge solutions.
2. Effect of bias filters – it is easy for you to ignore needs for which you cannot think of an easy solution because it is outside your experience or knowledge.

checklist

Build a checklist of questions to ask your customer(s) when you start to build the business case for the project:

- What changes are identified?
  - process changes?
  - behaviour changes?
- Are these just a 'quick fix' or a quantum leap?
- What does the customer believe is needed?
- Do all customers agree?
- Have the fundamental needs been separated from wishes?
- Are pre-determined solutions being proposed already?
- Has the end users perception of needs been identified?
- Have the needs been listed as primary, secondary and hopes?
- Has this list been prioritised and agreed with the customer?
- Can you turn the information into clear 'statements of need'?
- Can you use the needs analysis to derive a 'statement of requirements'?
- Will the customer agree with your statement of requirements?

Add any additional questions you can to this list:

____

____

____

____

____

____

____

____

You will need much of this data when you get to the next key step of defining the project.

the customer 'contract'

As project manager you have an obligation to turn your relationship with the customer into a form of contract. Often this is not a formal document signed by all parties but is an informal understanding. You may consider it appropriate to document some form of agreement on the obligations of yourself and the customer, focused on achieving the agreed outcomes. This will lead you to define the roles and responsibilities of both parties to the contract, to carry out the project work.

Many projects acquire a reputation for poor management when the reality is poor customer performance in fulfilling their obligations. Success is only possible if everyone involved fulfils their responsibilities and the customer cannot claim it as their right to act in complete independence. You must meet the customer requirements with constant attention to the triple constraints of project work – scope, cost and schedule. This is only possible if the customer acts promptly when necessary in resolving issues and giving approvals. Delays and cost overruns occur too easily if customer response is slow. It suggests the customer is not so interested in getting the results of the project on time.

watchpoint

Success is very dependent on your customer understanding and accepting the project process you will use. If the customer can accept your process and integrate this with the way they work you will avoid many potential roadblocks.

The project does not end with hand-over. You must check that the critical period after this phase is defined clearly for maintenance and service activities to check that the customer agrees who is responsible. Ensure these are design activities included in your project plan.

identifying the project constraints

The constraints limit all project activities. In today's business environment it is rare for you to have unlimited resources, funding and time to complete the work. The project may yield significantly reduced benefits if you provide the results at a time when the requirements or the market needs have changed dramatically.

Business and market needs are continually changing. Even with an internal project, late completion may lead others to conclude the whole effort was a waste of time, because of new requirements. Project 'drift' sets in and you face what seems like a never-ending project, trapped into acquiring a legacy of the 'project manager with the endless project'.

Constraints usually fall into categories:

- financial – project cost, capital costs, materials, revenue and resource costs;
- time – to deliver the results, the critical date when the results are needed;
- quality – the scope, specifications and standards to be achieved.

You need to explore each with your customer to gather the information you need to guarantee success. You will find that the customer will often be unable to answer your questions, arguing that it is part of the project work for you to uncover the answers.

watchpoint

Constraints are frequently regarded as fixed for the project life – it is valid to revisit the constraints again in the future. As climate conditions change so can the constraints.

For a further discussion on constraints and risks, refer to Chapter 7.

assumptions

It is inevitable at the start up of any project that you will make many assumptions about various aspects of the project. These are usually associated with the areas of greatest unknowns or complexity. Assumptions are potential sources of future road-blocks, so ensure that you do record them now and in the future as more get made.

At some point in your project you must validate every assumption or they will become issues to be resolved. The assumptions have no value later as excuses for failing to do something because either you or someone else forgot that it had been assumed and was never recorded. In addition the PST needs to know what assumptions have been made to help them with decision processing. It is easy in a climate that encourages you to get going with the project to ignore them and just take the view 'We'll deal with that later'.

watchpoint

Invalidated assumptions become issues that impact project progress and must be resolved.

the kick-off meeting

Hold a kick-off meeting. This meeting is the first time you collect together the team with other key people who have an interest in the project. It is an opportunity for you to demonstrate your ability to lead the project team. Good preparation is important to achieve the meeting purpose. Avoid diving into too much detail at this stage – that will come later. Focusing on one area in detail will divert the meeting and not fulfil the meeting purpose.

The project sponsor should chair and open the meeting to explain the strategic context of the proposed project. Explain why the project is important now and how it is ranked in contrast to other active projects. Your purpose is to gain as much information as possible at this stage by asking questions.

Issue an agenda for the meeting before the meeting to give attendees time to prepare. The customer and end user may bring two or three people to the meeting, but it is better to keep the group size down to a minimum where possible.

Some typical questions to ask at the kick-off meeting include:

background

- Why is the project necessary?
- What is the overall problem or opportunity being addressed?
- Has the current situation been explored and understood?
- Has a statement of requirements been derived from the needs list?
- Is this an old problem?
- How long has it existed?
- Who wants to change things?
- Have previous attempts (projects) been made to address this problem?
- What information exists about past attempts to fix things?
- What assumptions have been made?

context

- Is the project in line with current organisational strategy?
- Does the project form part of a program of projects?
- Will the project form part of a chain of linked projects or a program?
- What is the timescale of the project?
- Is there a business critical date to get the results?
- Will the results be of value to another customer or part of the organisation?

approach

- Have all the needs been identified and analysed?
- Has a statement of requirements been agreed?
- Are there predetermined solutions?
- What are these solutions?
- Is there a best option and a least worst option?
- Is there enough time to explore more than one option?
- Are there known checkpoints for project review other than the phase gates?
- What specialised skills are expected to be required for the project work?

objectives

- Are the project primary deliverables known?
- What does the customer need, want and wish to get from the project?
- Can these deliverables be clearly defined and specified?
- Does the end user agree with these deliverables?
- What does the end user need, want and wish to get from the project?
- What are the perceived project benefits?

- Have these benefits been quantified?
- Has a project budget been fixed?
- Is capital investment necessary?
- Has a capital expenditure request been initiated?
- Is time used for project work to be measured and costed?
- How were the costs derived?
- Has a cost/benefit analysis been carried out?
- Has a financial appraisal been carried out to establish payback?

constraints

- Have the project constraints been identified?
- Is there a time constraint for all or part of the deliverables list?
- Are there any financial constraints, for example, manufacture cost, project cost?
- Is there a financial payback constraint?
- Are there any known technical constraints, for example new or untried technology?
- Are there known resource constraints?
- Is the project team to be located together on one site?
- Is part of the work to be carried out at another site?
- Is part of the work to be carried out by sub-contractors or suppliers?
- Is there a preferred list of approved sub-contractors and suppliers?
- What existing specifications and standards are to be applied to the project?
- Are there any legal constraints that might affect the project work?
- Are there any security implications?
- Are there any operational constraints, for example, access to production areas/test equipment etc?
- Are there any Health and Safety constraints?

The data collected from these and other questions you can add will help you prepare a comprehensive business case. Your objective is to create a document that demonstrates:

- a clear understanding of the customer needs;
- what you can achieve to satisfy those needs,
- an assessment of the potential risks;
- what benefits the project could provide the organisation;
- an indication of the timescales involved;
- an assessment of the costs and return on investment involved.

The business case is not a one-off exercise as you will be required to review, validate and update, if appropriate, the contents at each phase gate until the project is complete.

recording essential information

You are not alone – no one likes having to record information in a regular and organised manner. Project work produces a large amount of data and it is important that you record essential material. One of the greatest timewasters in project work is repeating the recording of information in different formats, creating problems in its interpretation later.

Start off your project by avoiding the 'I'll do it my way' syndrome. Insist that the team keep all essential project records on a standard set of templates derived specifically for the purpose.

All these templates can be designed on a computer and networked for ease of completion from blank masters and given a standard distribution list. It is a good idea to give one of your team responsibility for configuration management to ensure there is always good version control of all documents.

5

the definition phase

the project brief and specification

The data you collect from the kick-off meeting should enable you to draw up a preliminary statement of the project objectives and the associated specifications. This step is often the most difficult because you must now formulate in realistic terms just what the project is about and what it has to achieve. This is the foundation of project definition.

The *project brief* is a document that summarises all the relevant facts about the project and is, therefore, a source of definitive information. The contents include:

- the project origins – a need or opportunity statement;
- the project rationale – why is it necessary now?
- the benefits of the project – to the customer and your organisation;
- the project budget if known at this stage;
- the current timescale and expected deadlines – subject always to detailed planning later.

This document is ideally just one piece of paper, but for larger projects it often takes the form of a report with many different sections. The former is best as it forces you and the team to focus on real facts and not hopes or wishes. Unfortunately during the start-up of most projects there is too much expression of hopes and the 'wish list'. You have to resolve this conflict to sort out what you can achieve in practice with current technology, experience and knowledge that is compatible with the statement of requirements.

The project specification is a term applied to many different types of documents and can include almost anything. Here the term specification describes any document that is an obligatory statement of procedures or processes that apply to the project. It is a statement of policy for the project.

watchpoint

The project brief is an executive summary of your project and when combined with the business case creates a project charter.

defining the project

You may ask at this point 'What is the difference between start-up and definition?'. The first is a data gathering activity. Definition is the process of turning the data into something that is no longer just a wish or a hope. Failure to give adequate time to this activity and derive all the relevant data for this foundation will lead to a poorly defined project with a considerably reduced chance of achieving a successful outcome.

what is necessary to define a project?

This definition phase is where many projects go wrong – often because there is no clear definition or it has remained confused with so many different stakeholder inputs. Remember successful definition must involve all the team at every step, to build their acceptance and commitment to the work of the project.

exercise

Having conducted a kick-off meeting what do you need to write down now to define your project? List what you consider is essential information:

Everyone has their own ideas about what constitutes a definition but your purpose here is to ensure that everyone understands:

- what you intend to provide from the project;
- what you do not intend to provide;
- when the outcomes are to be provided;
- what constraints you have identified;
- what risks are involved.

Is this what you have written down? Your objective now is to:

- use the data gathered about customer needs and expectations;
- turn these needs into requirements – what you believe satisfy the needs;
- derive a project definition to specify these requirements;
- ask your customer to approve this definition.

watchpoint

Don't spend time planning until the definition is agreed and approved by the customer and sponsor. This approval or 'sign-off' is essential to maintain their commitment to your project success.

Before you call the team together to define the project open the business-case document and review the initial data recorded. Some details may now have changed and you will need to draw any variances to the attention of the PST when you have completed the definition. The definition process is given in Figure 5.1.

a project organisation chart

Draw up a list to show who is involved in the project, recording:

- name and job title/position;
- location;
- contact telephone/fax number and e-mail address;
- date assigned to the project;
- name of their line manager and contact data;
- distribution list.

Date the document and issue to everyone who needs to know – this is an essential communication document for resource planning. It ensures there is clarity about who is committed to the project. Ensure the line managers of everyone in the team receive this information – they are stakeholders and need to confirm their commitment by agreeing to these new assignments.

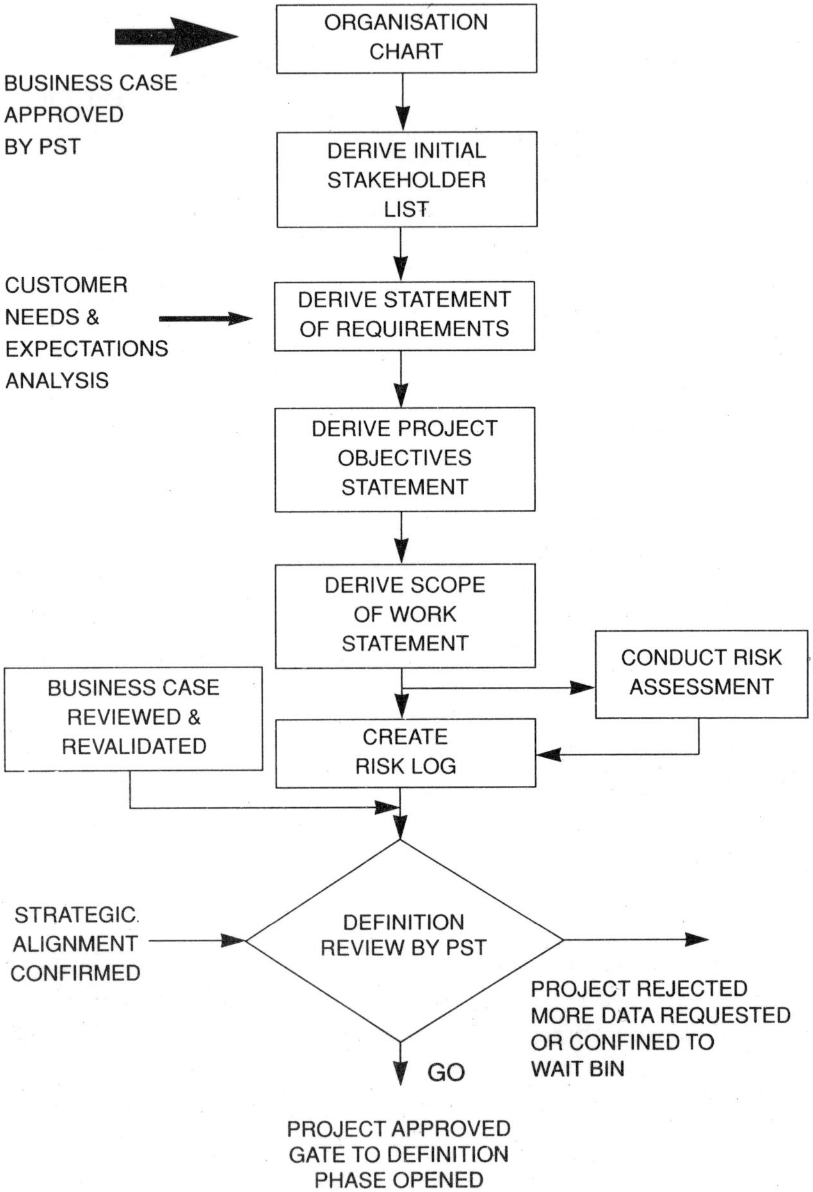

Figure 5.1 *The definition process*

a stakeholder list

Identify all those with an interest in the project – the stakeholders. The identification and management of stakeholders is a key activity for your success. It is suggested you read though Chapter 6 now before proceeding any further with definition. Create a stakeholder list, recording:

- name of stakeholder and job title/position;
- location and contact data (telephone/fax/e-mail);
- whether internal/external to your organisation;
- ranking of importance to the project (high, medium, low);
- current degree of support for the project (positive, negative?).

Date this document because it is subject to change as you review the list at regular intervals. Ensure the list is distributed to all stakeholders.

a statement of requirements

From the needs and expectations derived from your discussions with the stakeholders derive the data for this document. This must involve all the team to decide just what can be provided to satisfy the needs and may take several meetings. The document should record:

- needs and expectations identified and to whom attributed;
- how these needs can be met in practice;
- which needs cannot be satisfied yet and why;
- what assumptions have been made at this stage;
- what the project is about and what is not included.

The statement must always be qualified as being based on available information at the date of preparation as new data may become available later.

a project objectives statement

The information recorded here must be derived working with your customer recording:

- a statement of background;
- the project purpose – why are we doing this now?
- the overall project objective – in 25–30 words;
- the primary deliverables of the project with expected delivery dates;
- the primary benefits to be gained – quantified financially in the business case;
- the cost of the project;
- what skills are required – particularly those not currently available;
- any identified interfaces with other active projects.

Ensure all deliverables and benefits satisfy the SMART test:

SPECIFIC – clearly defined with completion criteria;
MEASURABLE – understood metrics are available to identify delivery;
ACHIEVABLE – within the current environment and skills available;
REALISTIC – not trying to get the impossible with many unknowns;
TIMEBOUND – is limited by a delivery date based on real need.

It is also valid to identify any important aspects of your proposed strategy for the project, for example:

- examining several options;
- using sub-contractors for part of the work (where skills are missing);
- using consultants for support and advice;
- re-using known methods, processes or technology.

If preferred this data can be included in the *scope of work statement.*

a scope of work statement

This is a convenient place to record other useful data and cross-references to past reports and relevant projects. The document also includes:

- the project boundary limits identified – what you are not going to do;
- the standards and specifications that are applicable;
- internal product specifications;
- external product specifications;
- mandatory standards imposed by legislation;
- process specifications;
- customer specifications;
- standard operating procedures;
- purchasing procedures;
- quality standards;
- testing specifications and procedures;
- sub-contract terms and conditions imposed on third parties;
- any exceptions to these standards;
- where the standards and specifications are kept for reference;
- how success is to be measured;
- assumptions made in the project.

The scope of work statement is a useful place to locate any other relevant information that supports and clarifies your definition.

a risk assessment

There are risks to all projects and *risk management* is the process of identifying and containing them to ensure your project is a success. What is a risk?

> ### definition
>
> In project work any event that could prevent the project realising the expectations of your stakeholders is a risk. A risk that happens becomes an *issue* that must receive prompt attention to maintain the project schedule on time.

A risk assessment at this stage of a project may kill the project – through identifying such a high level of risk compared to other potential projects that it is not good business sense to continue. Three fundamental categories of risks are always present:

- *business risks* – the viability and context of the project;
- *project risks* – associated with the technical aspects of the work to achieve the required outcomes;
- *process risks* – associated with the project process, procedures, tools and techniques employed to control the project.

As project manager, it is your obligation, working with your team to:

- identify and evaluate potential risks;
- obtain agreement to action plans to contain the risks;
- take the actions and monitor the results;
- promptly resolve any issues arising from risks that happen.

> **watchpoint**
>
> All projects inherently contain risk by default. Your success is dependent on how well you manage the risks throughout the project.

keep your head – don't go wild!

Project managers often complain that risk management is negative and an infinite process – you do not have to try too hard to come up with an enormous list of potential risks. There is no real value in listing risks you know just cannot be controlled by you or your team. Do not list 'acts of God' such as war, flood, earthquakes etc. Similarly many perceived risks in the economy and market place will have an eventual consequence for you but you cannot control these directly. Clearly some measure of judgement must be exercised when listing such risks to focus on those that may have a rapid and direct impact on your project. Then you can decide any mitigation action you could recommend if they seem likely to occur.

As we have identified earlier the management of risk is a key step for your success. Chapter 6 is devoted to the process involved in management of risks.

when is it necessary?

Risk management is a *continuous process* throughout the life cycle of the project and you must keep all the team focused on the risks:

- start now at the definition phase;
- it is essential to establishing the *definition*;
- compile a complete list as a *project risk log*.

Review the project risk log at regular intervals, normally monthly at project progress meetings. Focus this review on:

- any change in the potential impact or probability of identified risks;
- any risks changed from previously lower ranking are then subjected to closer examination;
- deriving contingency plans for either avoidance and/or damage limitation;
- adding any new risks identified to the list and assessing these for impact and probability.

A risk entered on the list is *never* removed, even if the time zone when it could occur has passed. Your list of risks is a source of valuable learning data for future projects and is a useful data source for deriving checklists.

getting your project definition approved

The final step in the definition process is to present your documented definition to the project sponsor and your customer for approval to go on to the planning phase. At the same time you should confirm the strategic alignment and review the business case to check there are no significant changes required that impact the viability of the project.

Start by checking you have done everything you can at this stage to clearly define the project by asking some questions:

- Is the project organisation clearly established?
- Is the customer identified?
- Are roles and responsibilities at all levels understood and accepted?
- Are project accountability and authority statements issued?
- Is the corporate and strategic context and priority of the project understood?

- Has a project organisation chart been prepared and issued?
- Has a statement of requirements been derived?
- Has the project stakeholder list been prepared and issued?
- Has a project need/purpose/opportunity statement been agreed?
- Has all the relevant background information been collected?
- Is there an agreed overall project objective statement agreed?
- Is there a business critical date for the completion of the project?
- Are the project deliverables clearly identified?
- Have the project benefits been established?
- Has the project approach and strategy been agreed?
- Is the project related to other projects?
- Have the project risks been identified and quantified so far?
- Has a project risk log been prepared?
- Has a scope of work statement been prepared?
- Have all assumptions made so far been documented clearly?
- Are existing communication procedures acceptable for the project?
- Has the alignment with current strategy been confirmed?
- Has the business case been reviewed and updated where necessary?

Now you can seek the approval of your sponsor and customer. If possible use the opportunity to hold a team and stakeholder meeting for this definition review. The sponsor will present the outcome to the PST for them to approve the definition and open the entry gate to the planning phase. This approval opens the way for planning effort to proceed.

6

managing the stakeholders

At the end of the project, who really decides whether it has been successful? Yes, it is the key stakeholders who will quickly make it clear to you if they consider the project meets their expectations. Conversely they are also quick to let you know if you have failed. They are frequently an ignored group and that justifies devoting this chapter to stakeholder management as a key step to good practice on the success ladder.

what is a stakeholder?

In Chapter 2 we identified the stakeholder as anyone who can find reason to have an interest, however direct or indirect in your project. These individuals who may act independently or represent groups consider they have a right to influence your project in some way. Ignore them at your peril.

---

exercise

Think about your last project and list all the people other than the project team who exerted some influence on the project objectives, work content or progress at some time during the project.

How many have you identified in just a few minutes? Now you can see that there could be many of these influencers working in the project environment. Although you may not readily accept the fact, you cannot avoid them and they will always exist.

---

watchpoint

It is an integral part of the project process to constantly manage your stakeholders for you to achieve success.

the importance of the stakeholders

Some of these people are key stakeholders for you because of the amount of influence they can exert. These demand the attention and focus of you and your team. It is essential to identify all the stakeholders as early as possible in the project life. Failure to enrol them in involvement to some degree may be fatal. Never underestimate the ability of any stakeholder to ruin your plans through use of their power.

All the stakeholders have an open and a closed or hidden agenda about what they expect from your project. You need to expose these expectations before you finalise the definition of the project and agree the scope. This is not easy when there is a political dimension affecting their needs and expectations – one need could be to hinder or stop the project! If your project includes some activities that impact on others and they see this is a change from their current situation, the consequence is a reaction. Exposing change often creates an initial emotive response before moving on to logical thinking.

Stakeholders can be positive, neutral or negative about what you are doing and it is important to understand their position.

The relative importance of each changes with time and the progress of the project and they may change their support to outright hindrance at any time if it benefits them as individuals. This is natural human behaviour to protect self-interest.

the two most important stakeholders

Clearly you should already know your two most important stakeholders – the customer and your project sponsor. If there is uncertainty here then start by removing any confusion before you go any further.

the project sponsor

This is normally the person who gave you responsibility for the project. In Chapter 1 we defined this person as having accountability for the project on behalf of the organisation. This is not just a nominal role because the individual happens to be a senior manager. Many projects run into difficulties because the sponsor does not fulfil the obligations of the role.

watchpoint

The involvement of the sponsor throughout the project is an essential success factor for your project as this individual has the authority and power to make decisions about money and the resources – the people that you need to get the work done.

The sponsor cannot be effective if the individual has no authority in the organisation. Most organisations today still maintain a reluctance to give their project managers enough authority to get the job done.

There are many occasions in project work when you will need to refer a decision to higher authority. You will also know that many issues that arise during the project will demand rapid response to avoid holding up the work. It is clearly easier and quicker to finalise a decision with one individual than go through the draconian process of submitting to a committee. The sponsor is accountable for the project and therefore is the appointed guardian of the project on behalf of the organisation. You should demand delegation of the authority you need to get the day to day work of the project done on time.

An effective sponsor can also provide you with a significant amount of support through:

- responding rapidly to issues requiring senior management decisions;
- sustaining the agreed priority of the project in the organisation;
- sustaining the project direction to avoid subtle enhancements of scope – scope 'creep';
- ensuring the project stays focused on the organisation's strategic needs;
- building a working relationship with the customer;
- influencing the peer group to provide cross-organisation resources and services on time for the project;
- demonstrating concern for success by visible leadership;
- influencing other stakeholders in the approval and sign-off of the phases of the project.

These are the essential responsibilities of the sponsor's role in project work.

build a relationship with your sponsor

Close collaborative working with your sponsor is clearly important for you to benefit from this support. Do recognise that the role is often perceived as just placing a name to a role with no consequent impact. You need to start out with the intention of building a good working relationship with your sponsor.

Agree that you will meet face to face regularly – preferably once a week, if only for 20 minutes. Managing issues is always preferably handled informally whenever possible.

Who is your sponsor?________________________________

Location: ____

Telephone no: ____________________________________

E-mail: ____

How frequently will you meet and where? ______________

the customer

Clearly identify who really is your customer and who is your main contact since you must start to build a working relationship with this individual. Many projects have multiple customers, outside or even inside the organisation. Customers have personal perceptions of what they want from your project and if there is a wide variance in these perceptions hostility and conflict may be generated. You need to use all your skills of diplomacy to influence such a group and identify the needs and expectations of each customer.

Who is your primary customer? _______________________

If you have more than one, who are they?________________

____

Who are the main contacts for each customer? ____________

____

____

____

Add contact details for each customer contact – e-mail, telephone number

Add these stakeholders to a standardised listing of all stakeholders.

One way to reduce the problems multiple customers create for you is to get them to agree that one of the group takes the role of *customer representative*. The customer representative is the key individual who has the necessary authority to take decisions affecting the project. Preferably this should not be a committee.

customer satisfaction

It is essential to recognise that customer expectations directly relate to customer satisfaction. Unfortunately there are degrees of satisfaction relating to the extent to which your customer perceives you understand their expectations and, what is more important, meet them with the results achieved. Fall short of these expectations and you will have unhappy customers.

Your goal is to have a delighted customer by providing all the expected results to an acceptable quality and standard. Fall short on the quality, scope or performance standards expected and you will only create a complaining customer. The complaining customer is potentially a lost customer in the future which is bad news for the organisation and your track record!

In addition the customer expects you to deliver on time – that is to an agreed schedule of delivery. This is effectively a promise by contract. Fail to deliver and you lose the respect of the customer and probably increase the project cost. This leaves you with a further issue of recovering the additional cost and a disgruntled customer is not too easy to convince that they should accept the increased cost.

Customers also expect you and your project team to serve them with professional competence. You must ensure the right people with experience and appropriate skills are assigned to the project work, behave in a cooperative and friendly manner and demonstrate a real concern to meet the customer's expectations.

who are the other stakeholders?

But where are the others? They are both inside your organisation and outside. It is a good idea to ask your sponsor and customer to get involved in the activity of stakeholder identification since some stakeholders impact both.

Start by thinking about the people:

- who you need to take with you through the project;
- who will be affected in some way by the project at any stage;
- who will be quietly watching what you are doing in the project.

Then start to list them in a standard format. Try to focus on individuals or the most likely representatives of groups not the group itself. This activity should be a team exercise and in the first pass put everyone you think of on your list. Ensure you agree with your sponsor what communication needs to occur to let others know you have started a new project and what it is intended to achieve. This is a valid reason for having a project charter and using this document for communication inside the organisation.

who will use the results?

Although the customer wants the results from the project, the customer is often not the person or group of people who will actually use the results on a day to day basis. You will need to have contact with the end users or a small representative group of the end users to check that you understand their needs and concerns about how the results will be used.

Some projects, by their nature have to be retained as confidential. When you are constrained by confidentiality this secrecy can create difficulties in stakeholder management. Take this into account as you are then forced to use other subtle means of information gathering later to assess your stakeholders.

stakeholder influence

As you start to build the stakeholder list for both the customer organisation and your organisation, consider:

- Who wants you to succeed?
- Who might want you to fail?
- Who will visibly support the project?
- Who will visibly hinder or oppose your project?
- Who will invisibly support the project?
- Who will invisibly hinder or oppose the project?
- Who will benefit from the project?
- Who will lose something because of the project?
- Whose success is impacted by the project?
- Whose success is enhanced by the project?

Depending on the type of project it may be valid to ask:

- Who can I ignore as the project progresses?
- Who can I not ignore as the project progresses?

Covert criticism or interference can quickly demotivate the team, destroy team spirit and promote conflict. Poor stakeholder control can lead to chaos, confusion and frustration in your team through this perceived interference. Now you have a more comprehensive listing you can ask two more questions:

- What needs to be known about each stakeholder?
- Where and how can this information be gathered?

gathering information about stakeholders

You will probably now have more stakeholders on your list than you ever thought possible. If you give them all equal time you will never get the project done so carefully examine the list and with your team agree:

- which stakeholders are critical to project success – key stakeholders;
- which stakeholders are best kept at a distance from the project;
- which stakeholders you are unable to influence at all.

Focus on the first category as a priority and for each ask:

- What exactly is their interest?
- Why are they interested?
- What are they expecting to gain?
- What do they need?
- How will the project affect them?
- Can they contribute experience, knowledge or specific skills?
- Are there likely to be hidden agendas and if so, what are they?
- What organisational authority does the stakeholder have?
- Will the project interfere with their operations?
- What might they lose because of the project?
- How could they hinder the project?

Add any additional questions you can that are relevant to your project.

Use the information you derive to decide what you must do next. Decide which stakeholders you need to meet to get the information you are lacking to confirm your conclusions about each. This may seem a formidable task and should not be underestimated about the time it will take. Remember you have a team and assign each member of the team one or more stakeholders to meet and gather information. You cannot afford to ignore these people. Give them respect in their role and you will get some surprises as you gather information. Your initial conclusions may be quite wrong so be prepared to receive new and unexpected data.

When you have gathered all the information you think necessary you will have a better idea who the most important stakeholders with whom to sustain contact are.

what happens next with stakeholders?

The list of stakeholders frequently changes as the project proceeds so expect new stakeholders to appear at any time.

> **watchpoint**
>
> It is important for your success to recognise that the stakeholder list is never static. Review the listing at regular intervals always adding any new information.

One final activity you can undertake adds more value to help you manage stakeholders more effectively. Take your list and categorise the stakeholders as one of the following:

- *decision maker* – one who provides resources or resolves issues;

- *direct influencer* – one who has a direct input to the project or is impacted by the project;
- *indirect influencer* – one with no direct input but who may be needed to agree some actions;
- *observer* – one who is not obviously affected by the project but may have an impact on their choice.

Summarise by deciding for each whether they are positive, neutral or negative about the project and with the team decide what actions you can take to turn negative and neutral stakeholders into positive and enthusiastic stakeholders. Finally think about communications again and decide how you intend to communicate with all these stakeholder groups you have created. Decide:

- what you need to tell them;
- how you will communicate with them;
- the frequency of the communication;
- how you will gather feedback.

Then tell them how and when they will receive this information but be careful not to overload them. Busy people will not read long reports and they need short, objective reports that are of interest to them individually.

The key stakeholders you have identified will be expected to contribute to the project by getting involved in the reviews you need to conduct with your sponsor at various stages of the project. Their continued commitment is important for your success, so ensure you inform them at an early stage of that expectation. Many of the stakeholders may not be familiar with this approach to sustained involvement throughout a project. Explain why this is important and that it will not demand a significant amount of time. Making them feel important is more likely to help rather than hinder you because of their remoteness.

7

managing the risks

Risk is an inherent property of any change activity and is considered exclusively as a future phenomenon. Risks may happen in project work but it is very difficult to write down any specific universal rules for managing all risks. Risk is subject to perception and we are all different in our approach.

why bother?

Risk management shows you the way to minimise or even avoid the 'show-stoppers' that can cost huge sums to correct. Many risks are well hidden away in the schedule and unless you look for them, will impact your efforts at a time you least want to know. There are many other benefits including:

- predicting the serious threats to your project before they happen;
- enabling mitigation actions to be implemented immediately;
- enabling contingency plans to be derived in advance;
- improved decision making in managing the project portfolio;

- providing valuable data for negotiating with suppliers and the market place;
- creating clear 'ownership' of the risks so they are carefully monitored;
- helping to create a 'no surprises' environment for the project;
- encouraging creativity and lateral thinking;
- encouraging decisive leadership rather than management of crisis.

Some will argue it is a costly activity – but never as costly as correcting the issues that occur later.

> **watchpoint**
>
> Risk management is not a 'utility', it is a vital and fundamental part of the project management process that impacts your probability of success.

The need for risk management is related to the degree of complexity,. innovation and amount of cross-functional working. Small projects confined to one functional area often use a small team and the need for risk management depends on the level of innovation involved. As Figure 7.1 shows increasing complexity and innovation with more cross-functional working increases the need for a structured approach to risk management.

understanding constraints

Constraints in a project are often confused with risks and we need to separate them. As a general rule regard the constraints as those things that are imposed on the project, knowingly or

INNOVATION	Very small projects Low complexity Single function	Small projects Low complexity Some cross-functional working	Large projects High complexity Multiple cross-functional working
HIGH	Organisation with small task force team limited maturity HIGH NEED FOR RISK MANAGEMENT	Organisation with critical projects small mature team HIGH NEED FOR RISK MANAGEMENT	Organisation with critical projects large mature team VERY HIGH NEED FOR RISK MANAGEMENT
LOW	Organisation with small teams [specialised] Limited maturity LOW NEED FOR RISK MANAGEMENT	Organisation with small mature team MEDIUM NEED FOR RISK MANAGEMENT	Organisation with large mature teams HIGH NEED FOR RISK MANAGEMENT

Figure 7.1 *The need for risk management*

unknowingly that you have no real control over. This means you have to live with the constraints throughout the life of the project and work around them to achieve your objectives. Constraints may help you bring the project to ground zero and the real world rather than be forced into a 'mission impossible'. To identify the key constraints ask some fundamental questions:

- What is the available budget?
- Is there a specific cash flow requirement to be satisfied?
- Is there a business critical date when the project must be completed?
- What minimum resources are required and are these available?

- Is there some skill and/or experience needed we do not have and have to learn as we go?
- What external resources are required and can these be funded?
- Is there specialised equipment required and will it be available?
- Is there consensus among senior management to proceed?
- Are there legal or statutory limitations now or imminent?

Ignore the constraints and you could easily find your project quickly descending into a quagmire of politics and indecision. Constraints usually fit into one of three types:

- Those that are known from the outset – examples are financial, time and quality or scope constraints. You know in advance what you are working with to achieve a successful outcome.
- Those that pop up during the project – examples are major scope changes, new budgets imposed or more frequently new constraints associated with resources. An example could be key team members assigned to you who turn out not to have the skills you expected.
- Those that arise from 'nodding commitment' – a nod is an outward sign of agreement to go ahead with a project when that individual has knowledge that may eventually constrain the project to almost certain failure.

After consideration of all the constraints a 'mission impossible' project will always remain a 'mission impossible' project unless the climate changes significantly.

identifying the risks

Use a team brainstorming session to initially identify risks during the definition phase of the project. You are seeking an answer to the question: 'What could go wrong at any time during this project?' The risk could be due to external or internal factors.

Remember to suspend all judgement during the brainstorming session – save the debates until you get to analyse the

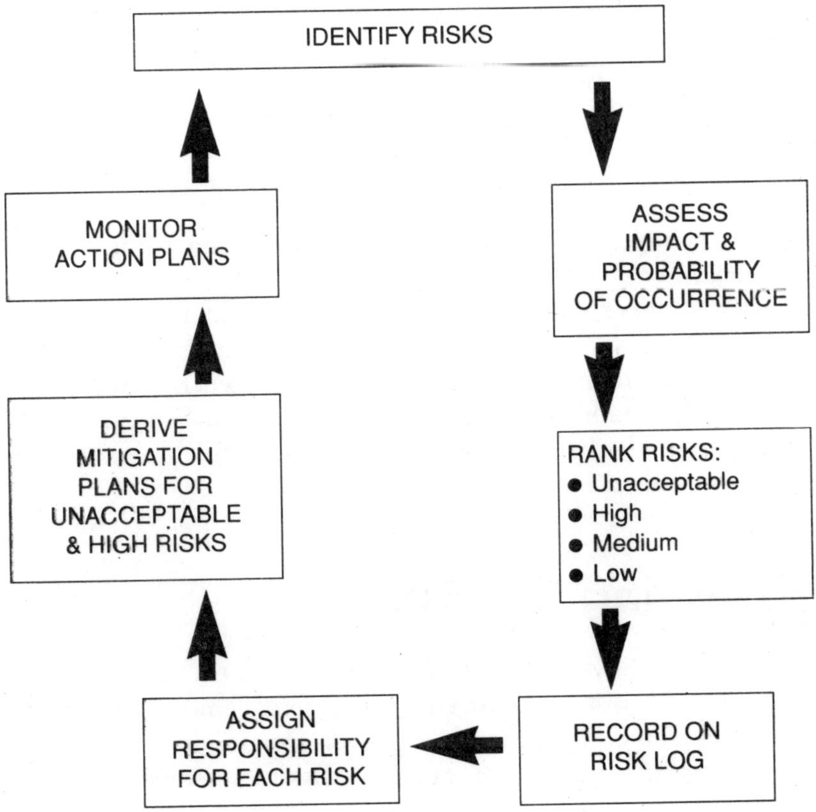

Figure 7.2 *The risk management process*

risks. It is preferable to conduct this part of the process after having had some dialogue with your key stakeholders. You can also use checklists that have been developed from data generated from past projects. Checklists are a convenient starting point to get the risk identification process going, but never regard the checklist as complete or perfect (or just 'good enough') and additional questions are always necessary.

Collect and review this list of risks and then conduct a preliminary analysis to eliminate duplicates and obvious rogues. It is useful during this analysis to ask what is impacted if the risk happens. It may be one of:

- *cost* – the overall cost of the work;
- *schedule* – the time the project will take;
- *scope* – the project deliverables and quality of the work.

If there is no impact on these three elements then ask if it really is a risk in your project.

This is where you must use judgement to focus the risks to those you consider are controllable in some way. This process often uncovers new constraints. Do not get fooled by the apparently small risks and ignore them. Small fish grow into big fish! Small risks can grow into 'project killers' if they are not observed and monitored.

assessing the risks

All projects have risks at the outset because of the many unknown factors, some of which you may remove during the planning stage. In practice risks disappear and new risks appear as the project progresses. Risk assessment requires answers to some key questions:

- What exactly is the risk?

- How serious is it as a threat to the project?
- What could be done to minimise its impact on success?

Having identified all the risks, review the list making sure none are duplicated, then record them on a project risk log giving each a number, name and the date identified. Then attempt to establish two characteristics for each risk:

- What is the probability of it happening – based on currently available data?
- What is the likely impact on the project if it happens?

This assessment can only be subjective based on the previous experience of you and your team but you should attempt to reach a consensus for each risk identified. Remember that *anything* that could go wrong and threaten the project is a potential risk and must not be ignored at this stage.

ranking of risks

When you have derived your list of risks use the team's experience to decide for each risk:

- The probability of occurrence on a scale of 1 to 9:
  - 1 is low – most unlikely to happen;
  - 9 is high – very high probability it will happen.
- The impact on the project if it does happen:
  - HIGH – significant effect on the schedule and project costs;
  - MEDIUM – less serious effect on the schedule, some effect on costs;
  - LOW – some effect on schedule, little effect on costs.

Remember this should be a team consensus decision using all the available information at the time. Once a set of risks has been assessed for impact and probability of occurrence you can rank them. Risks can be ranked using either a qualitative or quantitative approach. The simplest is a qualitative process using team judgement then fitting the results into a matrix. Either approach is based on the risk definitions.

risk definitions

Unacceptable risk – the project cannot proceed without some immediate actions to reduce this risk ranking to lower the probability of occurrence, either with alternative strategies or making significant decisions about cost, schedule or scope.

High risk – major impact on the project schedule and costs. Serious consequent impact on other related projects. Likely to affect a project milestone. Must be monitored regularly and carefully. Review possible mitigation actions you can take now to reduce the ranking or minimise the impact.

Medium risk – significant impact on the project with possible impact on other projects. Not expected to affect a project milestone. Review at each project meeting and assess ranking. Monitor regularly to ensure it does not turn into a *high risk*.

Low risk – not expected to have any serious impact in the project. Review regularly for ranking and monitor.

Clearly any projects allowed to proceed with many unacceptable risks are likely to be speculative, with serious potential for failure. By identifying such risks in this process you can alert your sponsor and senior management to what you consider may be a safer alternative strategy. Even a significant level of high risks may still be serious and need close management and control to achieve success.

Once you have given all your listed risks a probability and impact rating you can determine their ranking from the matrix below.

the risk matrix

Fitting the results into your matrix will probably suggest you should go back in the process and re-assess the initial ratings – especially if you have too many unacceptable or high risks! Some people are cautious and overrate risks, others are more optimistic and underrate the risks. Generally the latter types prevail and it is easy to go back and reduce the probability or impact on the high risks. Remember who has to manage the risks – *you and your team*, so underrating now is a poor excuse for failure later!

One difficulty often encountered is deciding the impact on the project, particularly during the early stages of the project

		IMPACT ON PROJECT		
		LOW	MEDIUM	HIGH
PROBABILITY OF OCCURRENCE	HIGH [7 – 9]	*Medium risk*	*High risk*	*Unacceptable risk*
	MEDIUM [4 – 6]	*Low risk*	*High risk*	*Unacceptable risk*
	LOW [1 – 3]	*Low risk*	*Medium risk*	*High risk*

Figure 7.3 *Risk ranking matrix*

before detailed planning has been conducted. The nature of the impact could cover a number of characteristics and it is sometimes easier to focus on the cost, schedule and scope in that order by asking:

- How does this risk impact the project cost?
- What is the potential impact on the schedule?
- What is the impact on our current scope?

Generally cost is preferred as a more definitive measure of impact as higher costs are related to schedule and/or scope in some manner. Deciding the impact of an increase in cost will help you to chose some mitigating actions that could include reducing the scope in order to maintain a schedule commitment later.

watchpoint

Even risks that do not apparently have an immediate direct impact on cost will eventually lead directly or indirectly to one or several risks with cost impact.

This exposure to potential project loss must be subject to analysis to enable effective decision making by the PST when considering continuation of the project. Record the ranking of all your risks on your project risk log.

what do I do now?

Any risks ranked 'unacceptable' must be closely analysed in more detail. If they could cause project failure decide if some changes to the definition are necessary to reduce the level of risk. If you can do something now to reduce the ranking then you must derive and implement an action plan now. No project should really continue with many such risks remaining. To derive action plans, record:

- a short description of the risk;
- when it is expected to occur;
- the probability assessed;
- what consequences are expected;
- what actions you will take if it happens;
- who will take the actions;
- who is responsible for monitoring the risk.

If you decide to change the ranking of a risk, record the change and issue the updated project risk log to the stakeholders.

monitoring risks

Once risks to the project have been identified and action plans derived then these must be monitored to make sure prompt action is taken when appropriate.

watchpoint

Risks change with time so careful monitoring is essential as the project proceeds, achieving success is dependent on effective risk monitoring.

Effective monitoring is a key activity towards achieving success. If risks happen they become issues that have a time-related cost impact. Unresolved issues do not disappear, they just accumulate and threaten to drown the whole project. You must act promptly to avoid this happening.

Assign each risk to a team member who has the knowledge and experience and responsibility for that part of the project most likely to be effected by the risk.

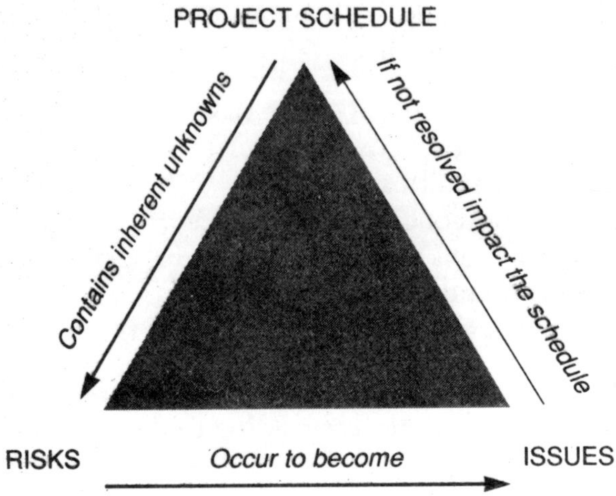

Figure 7.4 *Effect of risk*

Insert 'risk triggers' in the project plans to focus the peak period of possible occurrence. For example, if additional skilled extended team members are required in a certain part of the project, there is a risk they may not be available on time. Insert a trigger in the plan several weeks ahead of the timing of this need to focus actions to avoid the risk.

Create the 'look ahead watchlist' from those risks listed on the risk log. As the project proceeds you should review the risks at regular intervals and identify those risks that are expected or could occur in the next four to six weeks. Stress to the team the importance of watching for any signals that one or more of these risks are about to hit your project.

Finally, ensure you continue to look out for new risks and add this to the risk log using the same process. Unexpected issues will still happen and you may kick yourself later for not recognising them in advance. Most risks are (theoretically) predictable but you have many other things to think about so some will slip through unrecognised – until they strike! The power of hindsight is only valuable to protect the future.

8

planning the project

Successful planning does not just happen and many projects induce potential failure because of a perceived need to 'get on with doing the work'. Planning is a process of creating order out of apparent chaos, made complex by the environment in which you are operating. Give time to the planning process to avoid significant re-work later. Planning is about asking questions:

- What actions need to be done?
- When are these actions to be done?
- Who is going to do them?
- What equipment and tools are required?
- What is not going to be done?

The purpose is to convert the contents of the project definition documents into a time-based plan of action that everyone understands. This enables you to achieve the results on time, to the budgeted cost and to the desired level of quality. Project planning is carried out to:

- identify everything that needs to be done;
- reduce risks and uncertainty to a minimum;
- establish standards of performance;

- provide a structured basis for executing the work;
- establish procedures for effective control of the work;
- obtain the required outcomes in the minimum time.

Planning is a dynamic and continuous process to enable you to remain proactive throughout the project.

a common misconception

Planning is frequently regarded as just deriving a bar chart showing key activities against time – a form of schedule. This is just one part of the plan. Success with your project depends on a comprehensive plan that contains many other parts:

- a project schedule;
- a work breakdown with definitions of the work to be done;
- a resource analysis;
- a project budget;
- a communications plan;
- a quality/performance plan;
- risk management plans;
- an issue management process;
- a schedule of milestones.

At some time during the project all these are required and each should preferably be derived initially in the planning phase.

who needs to be involved?

You and your project core team together. Planning is essentially a participative activity that contributes to team building and creates team 'buy-in' to the plans derived – this commitment is essential to success. Before you start your first planning session, review the skills and experience of the team members. If appropriate, invite experts from other departments to join you, stressing this is not committing them to project work later and you value their input to your efforts. Persuade your project sponsor to attend and open the planning session, explaining the project strategic context, relevance and priority. Consider inviting some of your key stakeholders if they can add value.

where does planning start?

This is always a subject of debate and argument. If the customer has an expected completion date, should you fix the completion date and work backwards? Before going any further, some terms we use need to be defined:

definitions

A task – a (relatively) small piece of work carried out by one person.

An activity – a parcel of work of the project comprising several tasks, each of which may be carried out by different people.

Key stage – a collection of activities with measurable output, often confined to a functional area.

Concurrent activities – activities (or tasks) that are designed to be carried out in parallel, ie at the same time.

Series activities – activities (or tasks) that are designed to be carried out one after another, each strictly dependent on completion of the earlier activity.

Duration – the real time in working hours, days or weeks that a task or activity will take to complete.

Successful planning is a process of identifying sufficient detail to maximise concurrency and derive the shortest time to complete the project. You start by identifying the key stages of your project. These outputs may be deliverables or interim deliverables.

identifying the key stages

Two approaches are frequently employed, depending on the size and complexity of the work:

- *Top down* – listing all the interim and final deliverables of the project as outcomes from a collection of activities that forms a key stage.
- *Bottom up* – identifying as many activities as possible and the grouping related activities together to form the key stage.

Both methods are acceptable and successfully employed by project teams. The choice is personal preference. Top down is preferred for larger complex projects initially, followed by using the bottom-up method to identify all the tasks in each key stage.

top-down method

Write out the list of final deliverables as defined during project definition. Identify all the interim deliverables that must be produced to reach the point of completion of that deliverable. Remember that a deliverable or interim deliverable must be measurable – apply the SMART test again. This list will become your initial list of key stages, each having a defined output for another part of the project. Later we will examine how these are related to each other, as they are rarely just a set of series activities.

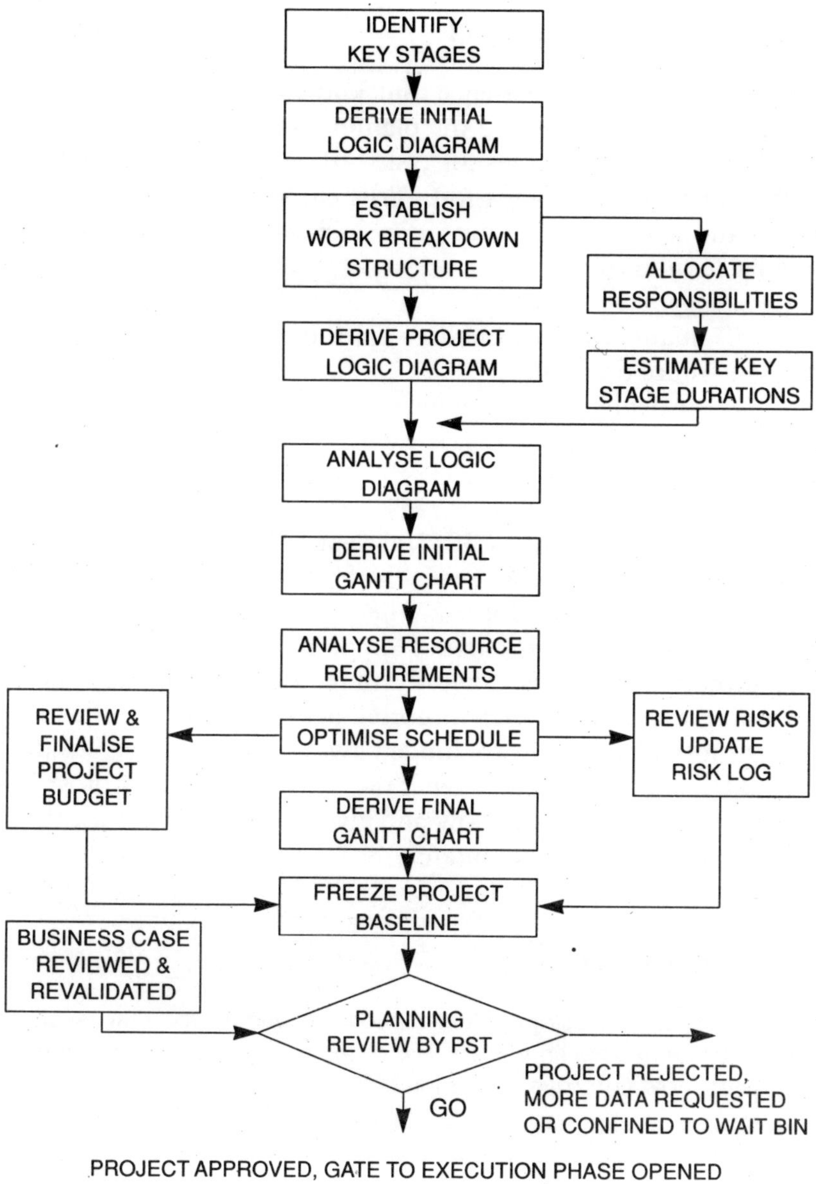

Figure 8.1 *The planning process*

bottom-up method

Use the collective experience and knowledge of your project team and others invited to the planning session, to identify the work as a list of activities (or tasks) to be done. This is carried out in a brainstorming session. Write everything down on a flip chart and when carrying out these sessions remember to follow the basic rules of:

- quantity before quality – even if the same tasks appear more than once;
- suspend all judgement – disallow any critical comments.

Reduce your task list to a reasonable number of activities, preferably in the range of 30–100 depending on the size of the project. These are the *key stages* of your project from which everything else is developed. When clustering activities, look for measurable outputs again. Do not get concerned that there are forgotten activities. The advantage of using the key stage planning approach is that forgotten activities lose significance for the moment as they are hidden away. You can return to the detail later. This approach generally helps you identify most of the possible concurrency now and gives you an activity list that is relatively easy to manipulate.

watchpoint

Do give this key stage identification adequate time – it is an investment to save time later! Two or three days dedicated to this process now can save weeks later.

using the key stages

Once the key stages are known and agreed you organise them into a logical sequence to maximise concurrency. There are some potential traps here for you: avoid considering real time or dates yet; and avoid assigning people or functions to the key stages. Both will lead you to create errors in the project logic. Your purpose is to generate logical dependency – which key stage is dependent on which.

The next step is to derive the *project logic diagram*. This is done using a technique known as taskboarding. Write each key stage on a separate small card or self-adhesive notelet sheet. Use these as parts of the project 'jigsaw' to build the picture. Arrange them in the right logical order either on a table, using a whiteboard or simply use the office wall. This is achieved by taking each key stage in turn and asking:

What must be completed before I can start this work?

Start with the first key stages that start from a card labelled START. Continue working from left to right until all the notelet sheets have been used. Connect all the notelets with arrows to show the logical flow of the project from start to finish. Some may require inputs from more than one key stage and others may create an output that is used as input for more than one key stage.

The advantage of this technique is that everyone can be involved. The graphic impact of the diagram developing makes each member of the team question and debate the validity of the logic as it grows. Developing the logic on the wall allows everyone to see it at the same time.

The step-by-step process to derive the logic is:

- time flows from LEFT to RIGHT;
- there is no TIMESCALE on the diagram;
- place a START notelet at the extreme left of the sheet;

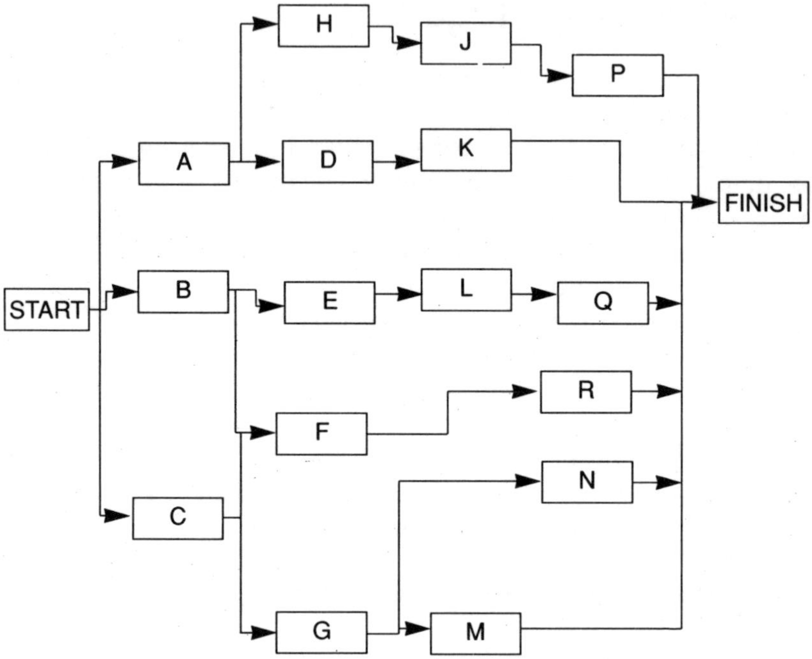

Figure 8.2 *The project logic diagram*

- place a FINISH notelet at the extreme right of the sheet;
- prepare a separate notelet for each key stage;
- start each key stage description with a verb (present tense);
- do not attempt to add durations for the key stage yet;
- use different colour notelets if appropriate for different functional activities;
- locate the notelets on the sheet in order of dependency – debate each one;
- when all the notelets are used, validate the dependencies – try working back;
- show the dependency links as FINISH to START relationships initially;

- do not take people doing the work into account – it can produce errors;
- draw in the dependency links with straight arrows ***in pencil***;
- avoid arrows crossing as it leads to confusion;
- label each key stage with an alphanumeric code: AB, AC, AD etc;
- do not use I or O (to avoid confusion with one or zero);
- when satisfied it is correct RECORD THE DEPENDENCIES;
- if appropriate, tape the notelets down to the sheet then roll it up for filing.

The golden rule of planning applies – always use a pencil and have an eraser handy!

Note that the logic diagram is continuous, in other words, every key stage has at least one arrow entering (an input dependency) and at least one arrow leaving (an output dependency).To assure integrity of the logic this rule must be maintained otherwise the plan will contain errors. Of course it is not unusual to find more than one arrow depicting dependency entering and leaving some key stages.

Note also that a fundamental property of the logic is that a new activity cannot logically start until all immediately previous activities finish. If you find on reviewing the logic that a following key stage can start earlier than the end of the previous key stage, the latter must be split to show that earlier dependence. The key to successful scheduling using this logic diagram is to ensure you have well defined dependencies.

the project work breakdown structure

The *work breakdown structure* (WBS), is a convenient means of graphically presenting the work of the project in a readily understandable format. The project key stages form the highest level of the WBS which is then used to show the detail at the lower levels of the project. You know that each key stage comprises many tasks identified at the start of planning and later this list will have to be validated. Expanding the WBS to the lower levels is the process of multi-layer planning you use throughout the project.

Note that:

1. The WBS does NOT show dependencies, just a task grouping under each key stage.
2. It is not time based – there is no time scale on the drawing.

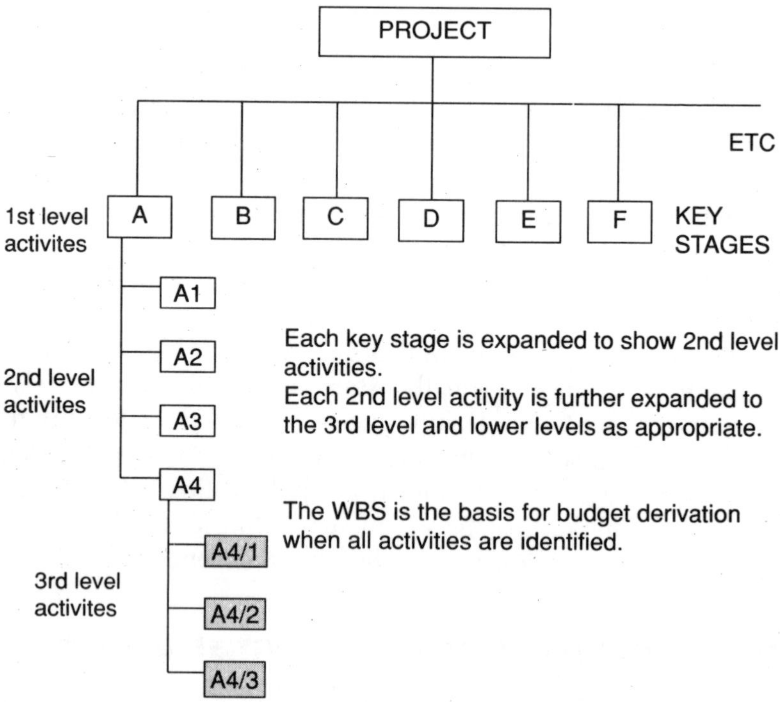

Figure 8.3 *The work breakdown structure*

The WBS is normally generated from project scheduling software once you have input the logic data.

allocating responsibility

Allocation of responsibility is essential to make sure the work is done on time and your objective is to distribute fairly and evenly the work in the team. Each of the key stages of the project needs to be owned by one of your team members. Persuade each member of the team to accept the role of *key stage owner* (KSO) for one or more key stages. The KSO accepts the obligation for his/her key stage to confirm:

- the work to be done is identified at the detailed task level;
- the dependencies are clearly identified;
- the estimates of durations are accurate and subject to constant scrutiny;
- the work gets done on time to the quality needed;
- the work conforms to quality assurance procedures and requirements;
- regular monitoring is maintained;
- regular accurate status reports are issued;
- problems and issues are alerted promptly to you.

watchpoint

Each key stage can only have one owner even if that person assigns some of the tasks involved. Split or multiple ownership leads to confusion and no ownership.

record your allocated responsibilities

Communication document for everyone involved including the line managers of the resources assigned to the project. As the plan develops more names are added as the extended team is identified for parts of the detailed work. Your *responsibility chart* should record:

- a list of the key stages and for each;
- who is responsible;
- who should be consulted for advice;
- who must be kept informed of progress;

and later add:

- planned start date;
- planned finish date;
- whether a critical activity.

Your reason for allocating these responsibilities is to assign the estimating of key stage durations to those people in your team who are most likely to have the appropriate experience or know who to consult to get the experienced inputs.

estimating

An estimate is a decision about how much time and resources are required to carry out a piece of work to acceptable standards of performance. This requires you to determine: the 'size' of the task or group of tasks, as determined from measurements if possible; and the amount of 'effort' required to complete the work. You must ask: how can the work be broken down? and can it be divided between two or more people?

Effort is measured in project time units – hours/days/weeks. Once the effort is known then optimise the resource needs, taking individual available time into account to determine the amount of effort required from each. Effort is a direct measure of a person's time to do a piece of work in normal workdays.

Duration is a conversion of effort taking into account the number of people involved, their capacities and an allowance for non-productive time. Since duration is measured in real working days this is never the same as the schedule, which has to take into account:

- non-available days for project work;
- non-working days – weekends;
- public and organisation holidays;
- staff holidays.

The first step for you is to derive some realistic durations and then apply these to a calendar to derive a schedule.

forecasting durations

As the duration of each key stage is the real time it will take to complete the work this is usually the most difficult part of the planning process. *It has been demonstrated many times that the majority of projects start with a schedule that has an inherent slippage of up to 30 per cent before you start the work*. This is largely due to poor estimating. The sources for accurate estimates are limited:

- experience of others;
- the expert view;
- historical data from other projects.

There is no substitute for experience. If similar work has been done before then you can ask others for their own previous experience and adjust the data for your project. It is a reasonable way to start but always take a cautious approach. The equation relating *effort* and *performance* is different for us all.

Who are the experts? There may be a few – or so they believe! Always ask questions about how reality compared with original estimates for some work. Check that the nature or content of the work did not change. You soon discover who is above average at estimating accurately.

contingencies

The purpose of contingencies is to attempt to quantify two additional factors:

1. The extent of uncertainty in the estimating process based on expected work content.
2. The risks associated with a particular piece of work.

Contingencies are not intended to cover changes to the project definition or objectives after they have been agreed with the stakeholders. Remember that most people include their own contingencies to protect themselves when asked for time estimates!

Agree the durations to be inserted in the plan with the team. These lead you to calculating the total project time with a projected completion date. Obviously there is a balance between the desired project completion date and the projected or forecast completion date based only on estimates. Somewhere in the middle there is an acceptable solution and only attention to detail and all the experience you can gather will help you to find it.

time limited scheduling and estimates

Imposed completion dates, given to you before any planning is carried out, always creates a conflict. This imposed date forces you to compress estimates to fit the date. To a limited degree this is acceptable as a target but too often this process moves you into a totally unreal situation where you are faced with 'mission impossible'. You must still prepare realistic estimates to derive a clear case and state:

- what you can deliver in the time;
- what you cannot deliver in the time;
- why you can only meet part of the objectives of the project.

You can then use your skill as a negotiator to arrive at an agreed solution!

guidelines for estimating

- Schedule full time team members at 3.5–4.0 working (productive) days per week (to allow for holidays, absences, training courses, etc).
- Include management time where appropriate as an additional 10 per cent.
- In planning, avoid splitting tasks between individuals.
- When tasks are split between two individuals do not reduce time by 50 per cent – allow time for communication and coordination.
- Take individual experience and ability into account.
- Allow time for cross-functional data transfer and responses.
- Build in time for unscheduled urgent tasks arising on other non-project activities.
- Build in spare time for problem solving and project meetings.

watchpoint

Any estimate is only as good as the data upon which it is based so like project risks, accept they may change with time as more data becomes available to you.

For each key stage keep a record of:

- the estimates you have finally decided;
- any assumptions made during estimating;
- where contingencies have been added;
- how much contingency has been added.

the critical path of your project

Critical path techniques have been in use on projects now for some 30 years, having proved their value as a tool for project scheduling and control. The fundamental purpose is to enable you to find the shortest possible time in which to complete your project. You can do this by inspection of the *logic diagram*.

Enter the durations on to your notelets in the logic diagram for each key stage. Begin at the START notelet and trace each possible route or path through the diagram to the FINISH notelet, adding the durations of all the key stages in the path. The path that has the highest number, that is, the longest duration, is the 'critical path' of your project and takes the least time to complete the project. All other paths are shorter. All the key stages on the critical path must, by definition, finish on time or the project schedule will slip.

This is where reality hits you – is the project total time what your customer actually expects? If it is a long way out, do not worry yet as most project managers expect this to happen. Remember your estimates are based on people's perceptions. Your objective is to attempt to compress the schedule to a time that is both real and achievable and satisfies your customer. Fortunately another valuable tool of project management is available to help you – *programme review and evaluation technique* (PERT for short). This tool allows you to analyse the logic diagram to confirm:

- the critical path – confirmation of your initial inspection;
- the start and finish times for all the key stages;
- the amount of 'spare time' available in the non-critical key stages.

The value of this data is to give you information for optimising the project schedule. This tool also provides you with the means to control the project work once this starts.

the PERT critical analysis technique

The PERT method of critical path planning and scheduling is the most commonly used technique for project management control. It is based on representing the activities in a project by boxes (or nodes) that contain essential information calculated about the project. The inter-dependencies between the activities are represented by arrows to show the flow of the project through its various paths in the logic diagram. The PERT diagram (sometimes referred to as a network) is identical to the logic diagram you derived earlier, each notelet for a key stage representing a node. The following paragraphs explain the conventional data stored in the node box.

The four corners of the node box are used to store the four characteristic times for the key stage. These are calculated times using the durations derived in estimating – remember to keep all durations in the same units.

The default or normal relationship used is FINISH to START. Under certain circumstances it is valid to impose constraints with the START to START or FINISH to FINISH relationships between activities, that is, pairs of activities are forced to start or finish together. You can impose a forced delay using a LAG between the START or FINISH of a predecessor activity and the START or FINISH of one or more successor activities. The forced start, or LEAD, is used to start a

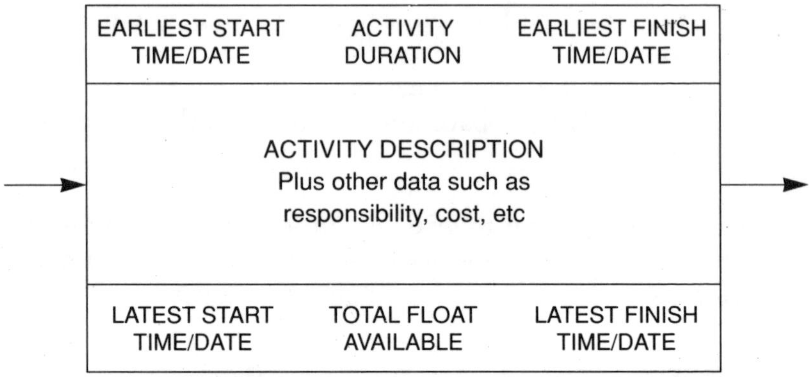

Figure 8.4 *The PERT node box*

SUCCESSOR ACTIVITY before the PREDECESSOR ACTIVITY is completed.

Lags and leads should be used with care – it is easy to become confused and introduce errors. Split an activity instead of using leads, to keep the diagram relatively easy to read and understand.

analysing the logic diagram

The analysis of the diagram is a simple logical process extending the initial calculation you made earlier to locate the critical path. Two steps are involved:

1. Adding durations from start to finish – the *forward pass*;
2. Subtracting the durations from finish to start – the *backward pass*.

In this way you and your team can quickly calculate the total project time and find those areas of the project where float or spare time exists.

using the PERT analysis data

At this point in the planning process you may be looking at a plan that is giving you a total project time considerably longer than you really want. Do not despair – yet! Do not go back and amend your time estimates. The next step is to convert the PERT data into a graphic format that is easier to work with and understand. This is the *Gantt chart* – a very useful tool for project work originally devised by Henry Gantt early in this century.

The chart is divided into two sections, a tabulated listing of the key stages and a graphic display where each key stage is represented by a rectangular bar. All the rectangles are located on a time-scaled grid to show their position in the schedule. It is useful to have both a project time scale bar and a calendar time scale bar across the top of the chart. This allows you to include the non-working days such as weekends and holidays. The key stages are listed on the left-hand side by convention, in order of their occurrence in the logic diagram (working from left to right).

You will note that the *total float time* is also shown on the chart as a line extension to those rectangles, or bars (the common term), on the right-hand end, that is, at the finish end of the bar. When you initially draw any Gantt chart the total float is *always* drawn at this end. The limit of total float is the limit of the time available for an activity or a group of activities in series, if the schedule is not to be threatened and extend the whole project. Total float is not cumulative in the whole diagram, only on a single path.

Of course *critical activities* have zero float and you can choose to highlight these with the use of colour. You can also include the dependency arrows on the chart between the start and finish of the dependent activities (ignoring the float zone). The Gantt chart can also show some other useful information:

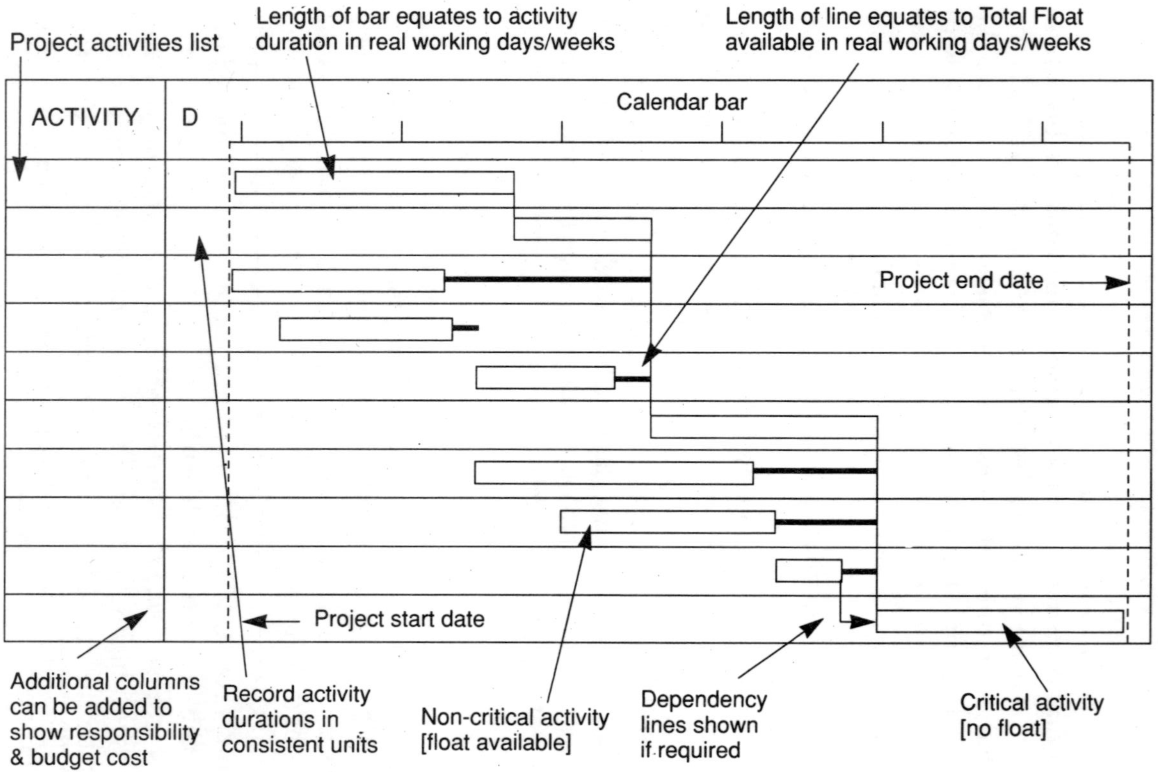

Figure 8.5 *The Gantt chart schedule*

- Milestones – special checkpoints usually indicated by a triangle or a diamond symbol;
- Project meetings – indicated by a filled circle or dot;
- Project reviews (ie financial/audit) – indicated by a filled square;
- Key decision points – often called 'gates'.

Remember to give a legend describing what the symbols mean!

The initial Gantt chart you produce at this stage is then optimised to reflect what you can achieve with available resources balanced with customer desires. This frequently involves compressing the schedule to reduce the time for the project.

> **watchpoint**
>
> If there are no resources to do the work in the time scheduled, the Gantt chart is a useless document expressing only hopes and wishes! Analyse the resource requirements for the tasks in the plan and then optimise the schedule.

using a computer

The optimisation may involve considerable reiteration to arrive at an acceptable solution – a process where project management software is very powerful. Small changes in the schedule are rapidly reflected in the chart and the logic simultaneously recalculated automatically. This allows you to carry out 'what if' analysis, viewing the impact of changing anything in your plan in a host of different ways. You can explore all available options you can think of to derive a finally acceptable schedule.

This process is necessary to convince your customer and the project sponsor just what is realistically possible if clear commitments of resources are made. Obviously this process is much more time consuming manually!

analyse resource requirements

Ask your KSOs to validate the task list in their respective key stages using the taskboarding technique. Much of the data will have been generated earlier but this now needs some closer analysis, particularly for the initial key stages. Identify the resources most likely to be assigned the work and then working with them as an extended team:

- review the initial task list;
- add to the tasks where necessary;
- analyse for the 'often forgotten tasks':
  - documentation;
  - approval times;
  - testing planning and development;
  - project reviews and gathering the data;
  - project meetings, replanting and planning reviews;
  - customer meetings and user group meetings;
  - negotiations with suppliers;
  - expediting and administration.

Suggest each key stage owner:

- derives a complete list of tasks in their key stage;
- produces a responsibility chart for each key stage;
- estimates the durations of all the tasks in the key stage;
- identifies the actual people who will carry out the work;
- confirms their commitment and availability.

It is good practice to derive the logic diagram for all the tasks inside each key stage. Then determine the critical path and the total float available in the tasks. Some of these tasks may be assigned milestone status later. This enables you to produce a Gantt chart for each key stage. In this way a detailed plan of the work for a particular part of the project is clearly defined by the people doing the work and it minimises misunderstandings about responsibility.

An advantage of this method is that the detailed work of a key stage does not need to be derived until a few weeks before the work starts. This allows the planning to incorporate any unexpected outputs from earlier key stages. In this way you continuously work to hold your plan dates, seek the required resources, validate your estimates and optimise your schedule to meet the total project time desired.

optimising your schedule

The schedule is always based on the calendar, taking into account the non-working days during the project. It involves taking decisions by consensus to maintain a balance between:

- the schedule – time;
- thc rcsources available – cost;
- performance – scope and quality.

The options available are fairly limited when optimising tradeoffs between these three to arrive at a solution.

watchpoint

Float time is not to be seen as an opportunity to stretch an activity to fill the available time. If you allow this to happen you create another critical activity by convention, so it is easy to turn everything critical by using up all float.

There is no perfect plan, only the best solution based on available information at the time. The options are:

- re-evaluate the dependencies in the logic for the key stages;
- review relationships – initially you used FINISH TO START, now examine if other types give an improvement;
- introduce LAGS and LEADS – with caution though;
- split key stages to get more concurrency;
- review assigned durations – review any contingencies added;
- review original estimates – realistically;
- seek more or different resources;
- seek to get current resource capacities increased – more time available;
- examine to ensure re-invention is minimised;
- reduce scope or quality or specifications – a last resort option.

watchpoint

Tell your team that float time is only used as a last resort with your consent (during the execution phase) to enable recovery planning when things go wrong.

When you are confident you have a realistic acceptable schedule update the key stage Gantt chart. Check your original project definition to ensure you have not ignored anything – particularly expected dates quoted and assumptions made. Present this schedule informally to your customer and project sponsor to confirm if it is acceptable. If not, then you must seek alternative solutions through further optimisation. If the schedule is nominally agreed you can proceed to the final steps of planning before launching the actual work.

review the project risk log

Review all the risks identified during the project definition phase. Ask:

- Have any changed status?
- Are there any new HIGH risks?
- Are there any new risks identified from planning?
- Examine your schedule to identify possible risks:
  - tasks on the critical path (and inside a key stage);
  - tasks with a long duration (low capacity factors?);
  - tasks succeeding a merge of two or more activities;
  - tasks with little float left (where is the float?);
  - tasks dependent on third parties;
  - lags and leads;
  - start to start relationships;
  - tasks using several people;
  - complex tasks;
  - anything involving a steep learning curve;
  - tasks using new or unproved technology.

Prepare new action plans for any new HIGH risks identified or those that have moved up in ranking. Assign responsibilities for day to day monitoring of risks to the KSOs. Avoiding a risk is better than a damage limitation exercise later!

review the project budget

Begin by updating the project WBS with all the lower level detail – or at least as much as you can at this stage. This is the easiest way to work out the cost of each based on:

- capital equipment costs;
- resource direct costs – based on cost rates;
- revenue costs for the project team;
- indirect costs – chargeable overheads, etc.

With the costs of each key stage identified you can produce an *operating budget* – the real budget for project control purposes. If it varies significantly to the original *approved budget* in the business case then this variance must be investigated and the conflict resolved. If an increased cost is identified then the customer will need to be consulted for approval. Prepare for this discussion by deriving some alternate options as you did when optimising the schedule earlier. Keep a record of all costs for control measurement and variance analysis.

freezing the baseline schedule

Review the schedule you have now derived and make sure you have not forgotten anything! This is soon to be frozen as the baseline schedule. Everything that happens in future will be measured against this schedule. You will need to present the plan documents to your sponsor and then the customer for approval and acceptance. Use this checklist to review the plans with the team and ensure you have not forgotten anything:

- ☐ Is the project definition still completely valid?
- ☐ Is the scope of work statement still valid?
- ☐ Has the project manager's authority been confirmed in writing?
- ☐ Are all stakeholders identified?
- ☐ Does the team understand who manages the stakeholders?
- ☐ Is the WBS developed as far as practicable?
- ☐ Does the WBS include all administration tasks?
- ☐ Are customer and sign-off checkpoint meetings included?
- ☐ Is the current critical path established and agreed?
- ☐ Are all key stages allocated for responsibility?
- ☐ Are KSOs clear about their responsibilities?
- ☐ Is the project risk log complete and up to date?

- ☐ Are duration estimations recorded?
- ☐ Are resource loadings and capacities optimised and agreed?
- ☐ Does the Gantt chart reflect an agreed schedule?
- ☐ Has the project operating budget been approved?
- ☐ Have supporting plans (as required) been derived for quality assurance, communication, configuration management?
- ☐ Does the team include all the skills needed?
- ☐ Has action been taken to acquire unavailable skills needed for the project?
- ☐ Are the team members working well together?
- ☐ Have any conflicts been resolved promptly?

Seeking approval to launch

You have now completed the planning phase as far as necessary before launching the project work. At this point plan documentation comprises:

- a list of key stages;
- the project logic diagram;
- a project key stage responsibility chart;
- responsibility charts, if appropriate, for each key stage;
- a record of estimates for all the key stages;
- an optimised project Gantt chart for the key stages;
- Gantt charts for the early key stages or all of them;
- an updated and reviewed project risk log;
- a project operating budget;
- other plan documents as required.

Now present these documents to your customer and project sponsor for signature of approval to proceed, opening the gate into the next phase, launching the actual project execution.

9

launching and executing the project

There are still a few things to think about before you hit the 'GO' button and launch into execution of the work. You need to validate all those promises of resource availability and confirm the reporting and communication processes.

preparing for project execution

confirming resource commitments

Create the initial work plans by asking the key stage owners (KSOs) to verify their task lists, making sure they have not forgotten any tasks. You can use a standard format to record these task lists with a clear identification who is responsible for completing each task in the key stage. It is useful to also record:

- the key stage code as recorded on the WBS;
- the key stage schedule start and end dates, whether it is critical and calculated float;

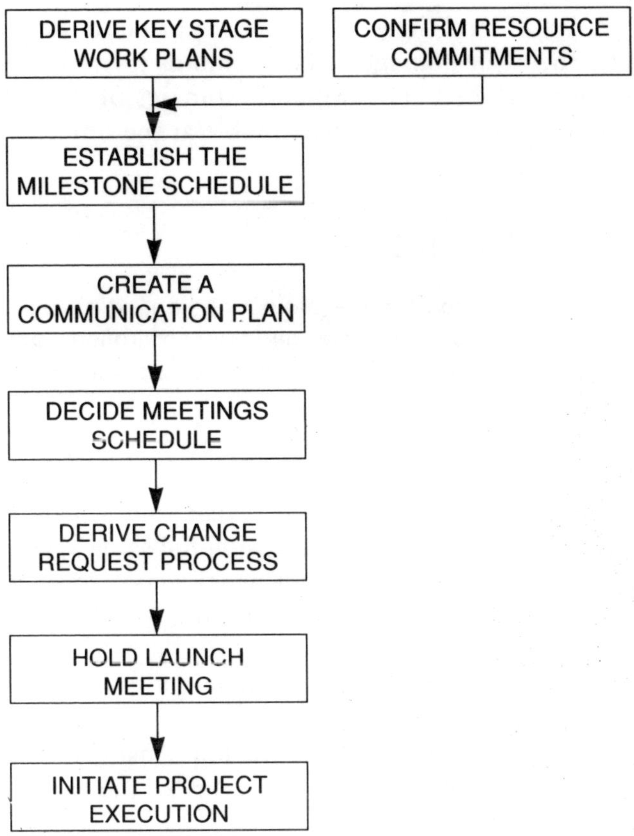

Figure 9.1 *The launch process*

- the duration of each task in the key stage using consistent units;
- the amount of float in each task if this has been calculated;
- the plan START and END dates for each task;
- a record of the ACTUAL START and END dates for each task.

Copy and send the work plans produced to the people involved and their line managers. This reminds them of the contract they have concluded. The original estimates of duration are only as good as the information available at the time.

watchpoint

In looking ahead in the project at the next pieces of work to be done, always revisit and validate the duration estimates. Amend these in advance rather than find out later that the estimates were wrong.

If the result is not acceptable revisit your schedule and if appropriate optimise the schedule using the same approach as before. Your choices are limited but usually enough to come up with a satisfactory and acceptable solution:

- seek more resource capacity;
- obtain more resources;
- review and modify the logic inside the key stage;
- amend the scope or quality of the work.

Although this may seem to be a time consuming activity, you are only asking your team to use a consistent and disciplined approach to work planning. You do not need to produce all the work plans at the outset, just those for the first few key stages. As the project continues, you can work proactively to prepare more work plans, taking into full account everything that has happened in the project. This is known as 'layering the plan' as the project proceeds.

establish a milestone schedule

Earlier we showed how risks and issues relate to the project schedule. The *milestones* are an integral part of this schedule so they are subject to the same risks and issues:

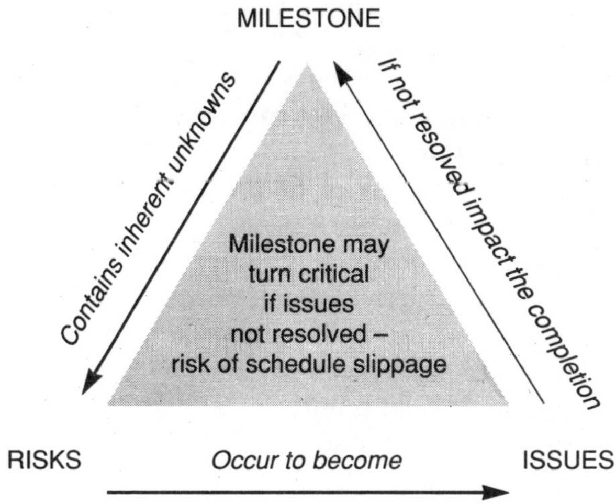

Figure 9.2 *Milestone and risks*

The milestones are all the significant events that are due to occur during the execution of the project. The milestone is a flag or signal at some clearly defined point in the project. The milestone is a point of control, placing target points in the project schedule for certain events to be signed off as completed. Milestones are either 100 per cent complete or not complete – there is no partial completion!

watchpoint

A milestone is a significant, measurable event in the project life cycle. Think of the milestones as the 'marker posts' to show the route to the finishing post – project completion.

Some of the common events given the status of project milestones are:

- completion of a key task, for example, providing output to third parties;
- completion of one of the project deliverables;
- stage generation of benefits;
- completion of a third party significant event, for example, acceptance tests;
- completion of third party activity, for example, delivery of equipment or data;
- a financial audit point;
- a project audit point;
- a quality audit;
- completion of a significant stage of work (possibly a critical element);
- a significant decision point, for example, abort the project;
- completion of a project stage to release further funding.

watchpoint

For a successful project you must reach each milestone on time or explain why a slippage has occurred. Then look for ways to recover lost time.

The frequency of milestones in a network must be sufficient for effective control. Record the milestones on a schedule listing and on the Gantt chart. For effective control ALL milestones must be measurable with clearly established metrics – apply the SMART test you applied to deliverables earlier.

have a communication plan

Poor communication is a major source of conflict so give this serious attention before you start the project work. Ask yourself:

- who needs to know;
- what do they need to know;
- how much do they need to know;
- how often must they be informed.

Establish distribution list(s) as appropriate but avoid generating large volumes of paper. Decide the ground rules you will impose on everyone to get prompt feedback of the prevailing situation with the work in progress. Effective monitoring and tracking of the project is dependent on good communication in the team, between you and the team and your key stakeholders. You need prompt feedback about:

- current progress of the active tasks;
- problems encountered with the work;
- problems anticipated with work waiting to be done;
- technical difficulties being encountered.

project status reports

Your key stakeholders expect to receive regular status reports. Decide the frequency and format of these with your customer and sponsor. Clearly define any metrics you will use and decide just what data you need to receive about the status of the project, such as:

- what has been completed;
- what has not been completed and why;
- what is being done about the incomplete work;
- what problems remain unsolved;
- what needs to be done about these unsolved problems and when;
- what difficulties are anticipated in the work waiting to be done.

watchpoint

It is appropriate to design a single page standard template for reporting project progress to ensure consistency and focus. Require these reports to be issued to you on a regular cycle of one, two or three weeks as appropriate.

This template should at least record:

- a concise summary of overall progress;
- a list of milestones due to be completed since the last report and their current status, ie on time or late;
- a list of milestones with dates due in the next reporting period;
- actions set in place to correct any slipped milestones;
- forecasts for the project completion based on current information;
- reasons for any revision to earlier forecasts to completion;
- changes to the project risk log;
- any issues (problems) outstanding still waiting for resolution;
- costs to date compared to the budget.

No one likes to hear bad news, but the sooner it is exposed the quicker you can react to limit the damages and take corrective action. You can use this template at any level in the project – the KSOs reporting to you and your reports to the customer and sponsor. Good teamwork is directly related to effective and regular communication.

what meetings do I need?

The different meetings you may need include:

- one to one meetings with the project sponsor;
- one to one meetings with your team members;
- project progress meetings with the team;
- problem solving meetings;
- meetings with particular stakeholders – the customer;
- project review meetings with other stakeholders.

All are necessary at different frequencies throughout the project and all must have a clear purpose. The one to one meetings are very important to maintain close contact with your project sponsor and the members of your team helping you to:

- know and understand these people as individuals;
- give and receive information at a personal level;
- discuss problems of a more personal nature that impact on performance;
- give guidance and support;
- coach team members;
- recognise their efforts;
- encourage and support personal development.

Problem solving meetings tend to be held as problems arise, involving specific people, which may not mean the whole team. Do not mix problem solving with progress or team meetings as the discussion easily gets out of control and the meeting becomes diverted from the purpose.

Agree a schedule of project progress meetings, throughout the whole project, showing the schedule dates on the key stage Gantt chart. If you have nothing to discuss, cancel or postpone any meeting.

handling project changes

However good your plans, there are certain to be some unexpected surprises. Minor changes appear during monitoring and are controlled by prompt reaction and taking corrective measures. Significant change is much more serious and needs closer scrutiny. These changes can come from:

- the customer;
- the end user;
- the sponsor;
- technical problems.

All can lead to replanning of the project and scope changes. Any change that is expected to create a replanning activity and affect the total project time as currently scheduled must be handled in a formal manner. Always examine:

- the source of the change request;
- why is it necessary;
- the benefits from making the change;
- the consequences of doing nothing at this stage;
- the cost impact of making the change;
- the effect on project constraints;
- the effect on resource needs;
- the increase or decrease in project risks;
- the effect on the objectives and scope of the project.

Major change can have a demotivating effect on the team unless it is something they have sought in the interests of the project. A major change on one project could have serious impact on the resource availability for another project.

> **watchpoint**
>
> The customer and the project sponsor must approve all major changes before action is taken to replan.

Derive alternative solutions and examine the consequences and risks before seeking an agreement with the customer. Formalise change requests – this often makes many requests for changes suddenly disappear!

hold a launch meeting

Now you can launch the project. The launch meeting is a milestone in your project after which all project work starts. Collect together all the important people who are involved with your project and explain the plans in some detail. Prepare yourself and your team well for the meeting. This is an important opportunity for you to explain the plan and the areas of high risk to achieving success. You are looking for acceptance from all those present that the project is well planned. You must convince them that with their cooperation you can achieve the objectives. No one can later complain they do not understand the project plan or what you are trying to achieve.

maintaining plan integrity

New information inevitably comes in to the team members

after the work starts. This can be quite casual through informal meetings in the corridor, staff restaurant or even the car park, or through lower level sources in the customer's organisation. The input is also intentional on occasions and could have profound effects on the work, the schedule and team motivation.

You must prevent any input amending the plans, increasing the scope or creating more work than necessary and remind team members to inform you immediately of such situations. You are asking your team to keep you informed of progress, so when additional information appears you (and the team members) must ask:

- Where does the information come from?
- Why was it not exposed before?
- Who has decided it is relevant now?
- Is the information accurate and realistic?
- Is there some hidden agenda associated with the timing?
- What impact does it have on the plan and schedule?
- Does this change the project objectives, deliverables or benefits?

Project work can be seriously constrained, or even sabotaged by the subtle transfer of erroneous information to a team member. A complete absence of information when it is due to appear can have similar sinister origins. Always be openly prepared to consider changes to your plan when essential. If the information and data essential to the project work is confused by mixed messages from different people then you face potential conflicts and confusion. Prepare your team for these events because they are certain to occur at some time in the project's life – if you have not experienced them already! Establish an early warning system to ensure you get rapid feedback about what has happened and what needs to happen. This provides you with the information to control the project.

the control environment

Control of a project environment involves three operating modes:

- *measuring* – determining progress by formal and informal reporting;
- *evaluating* – determining cause of deviations from the plan;
- *correcting* – taking actions to correct.

Control is associated with the present, so reporting is time-sensitive to allow you to take prompt corrective action.

> **watchpoint**
>
> If all reporting is historical and a considerable time after the event, then you cannot successfully control your project.

The communication processes you established during the project launch are designed to give on-time visibility to significant events.

design your control system

The purpose is to ensure that you and the team always have the information to make an accurate assessment of progress and keep the project under control.

The best control system is the simplest. The basic inputs to control are the schedule and the actual results observed and measured by the team. The comparison activity should show whether the project is on track and everything is going according to plan. If this is true you can update the project

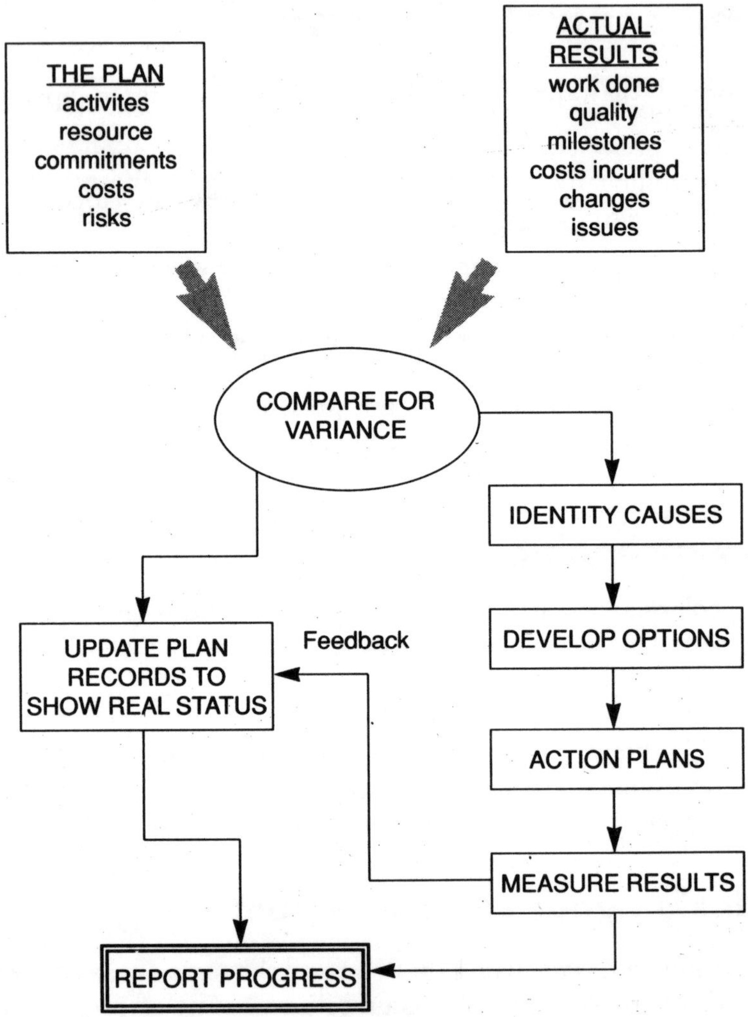

Figure 9.3 *The project control system*

records and charts and report progress and any slippage to your customer and project sponsor.

Corrective action plans are of no value unless you give particular attention to follow up and checking that actions have been completed and produced the desired result. Controlling the project means managing the many problems that arise to maintain the project baseline schedule through:

- monitoring the work – observing and checking what is happening;
- identifying and resolving the issues that arise;
- tracking the project – comparing with the plan and updating the records.

watchpoint

The simplest way to track your project is to use specific control points – the project milestones. Focus the team on these marker points, stressing the importance of maintaining the dates and that you must know if any milestone date is expected to slip.

Remind them that the total float is not spare time for them to use as they like without reference to you. Keep the project records up to date with a regular check and update of:

- the organisation chart;
- the stakeholder list;
- the key stage responsibility charts;
- the key stage Gantt chart;
- the work plans;
- the project risk log;
- the project issue log.

Using a project management software package can help you maintain your project data – once you are familiar with its many features!

Keeping the project records up to date is an obligation you must fulfil. You could be moved to another project at any time and someone else has to take over. Do ensure that the legacy you leave behind is a good one, otherwise you will continually be subject to queries and requests that interfere with your new role.

monitoring the progress

This is not done by waiting for progress reports to be issued. You need to walk about, observe and have conversations! This is your data gathering process, which if done effectively is far more useful then any written report. Confidence in progress reports only comes from verifying these from time to time. This obliges you to monitor both the team performance and the stakeholders' performance. Monitoring is a checking activity to:

- talk to the team members to find out directly how things are going;
- encourage the team and show you care about them and their work;
- check that promised resources are in fact working on project tasks;
- rapidly learn about concerns and difficulties.

Excessive monitoring may be perceived as interference, so there is a fine balance between the two extremes.

watchpoint

Regular monitoring with personal contact demonstrates your concern for success and reinforces messages about watching out for new risks or anticipating future problems.

measuring the progress

Ask the team how progress is easily measured. They must agree:

- the output criteria for each activity;
- the performance metrics to use and confirm completion;
- the frequency of measuring and recording;
- how to report the progress deviations or exceptions.

If unusual or unexpected results appear you need to be informed promptly so that corrective action can be decided. Remind the team to watch out for the risks that are particularly relevant at each stage of the work – these can produce real roadblocks.

managing the issues arising

The purpose of an *issue management process* is to make sure all risks that happen are resolved promptly to avoid and/or limit damage to your project. Generally issues do not go away and success depends on this prompt action.

> **definition**
>
> An *issue* is any event or series of related events (that may have been previously identified as a *risk*) that have become an active problem causing a threat to the integrity of a project and/or related projects.

Managing issues is similar to managing the original risks, requiring you to keep records of all issues that occur, and

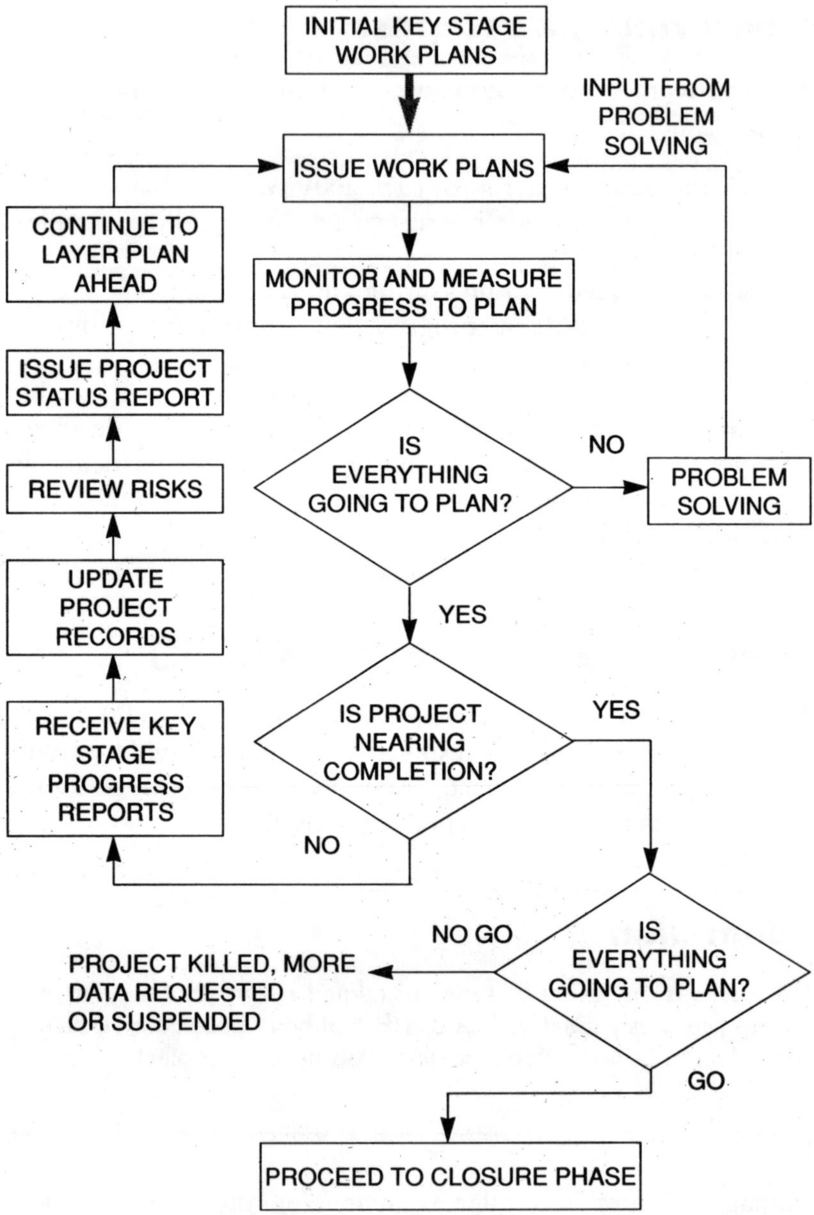

Figure 9.4 *The monitoring process*

ensure action planning is promptly used to resolve the issues. Your concern must be to get an action plan moving quickly. Do not over-react and action the first idea that jumps to mind. This is not always the best solution so utilise the team's expertise in deriving an answer to the problem. Keep a record of all significant issues as they happen giving:

- issue name and source;
- who owns it for resolution;
- which parts of the project are affected;
- who is responsible for action plans to resolve the problem;
- a record of current ranking;
- a record of when action is complete.

Design a template similar to the project risk log. Issues are identified and tracked through regular monitoring.

ranking the issues

You will probably resolve most of the issues but some will need the authority of the sponsor. Ranking an issue clearly identifies who is responsible for deriving the action plan. Issues raised are ranked according to their impact and anticipated consequences by assigning a RED, YELLOW or GREEN FLAG.

RED FLAG: Major issue having serious consequences for the project. Prompt action needed to implement a decision to resolve.
Responsibility: **PST or sponsor**

YELLOW FLAG: Significant impact on the project and/or other projects. Unless resolved promptly will cause delays to milestones. Becomes **RED** if action delayed more than two or three days.
Responsibility: **Project sponsor**

GREEN FLAG: Consequences limited to confined area of the project and unlikely to impact other projects. Becomes **YELLOW** if not resolved in time to avoid project slippage.
Responsibility: **Project manager**

Outstanding issues are identified when reporting progress of the project. You must also ensure that the ranking of any issue has not changed. It is important to keep your key stakeholders informed on progress with resolving issues, invoking their active support when necessary in the interests of the project.

resolving issues

Remember it is the issues that are the 'success killers' interfering with your target of maintaining the project schedule so apart from prompt reaction, ensure you:

- involve the team in solving problems;
- use additional expertise where appropriate;
- identify areas of the project affected:
  - consequences as perceived now;
  - consequences in the future if not resolved;
  - options to resolve the problem and for each option:
  - cost and resource implications;
  - effects on the project schedule;
  - effects on scope – quality;
  - risks associated and new risks created;
  - future issues identified/uncovered.

Always confirm that responsibility is clearly allocated for actions:

- Who is responsible?
- When must the action be completed?
- Who must be kept informed of progress?
- Who monitors – during and after?

watchpoint

Issues affecting non-critical activities cannot be ignored. Slippage of such activities can cause the critical path to move affecting the whole schedule.

tracking your project

Tracking is the process by which the project progress is measured through monitoring to ensure that changes to the schedule caused by issues or the customer are promptly acted upon and that the reported progress data is used to update the plan charts and records in the project file.

Your starting point is the baseline against which the variances are identified. The baseline for all tracking is the project baseline schedule and other plan documents devised and frozen before implementation, when all key stages are fixed. The project baseline should remain unchanged throughout the project. As the work is done you mark progress on the chart by filling in the bars to show the amount of work completed.

If a key stage is late starting, takes longer to complete, or the finish suffers a delay, this is shown clearly on the chart. The original position of the bar on the chart is unchanged as the baseline. Modifications to the schedule are recorded as they occur to enable the experience to be logged for future projects. This may move one or more activities away from the original baseline position, modifying the project strategy for a reason. Keeping the baseline unchanged forces you to fully document any changes to the plan and schedule and later evaluate the key learning points from all these changes that occur.

If any of these modifications cause a slippage to critical key stages then the project completion will be delayed. You then face the difficult task of recovery planning to restore the original project schedule or persuade the customer to accept

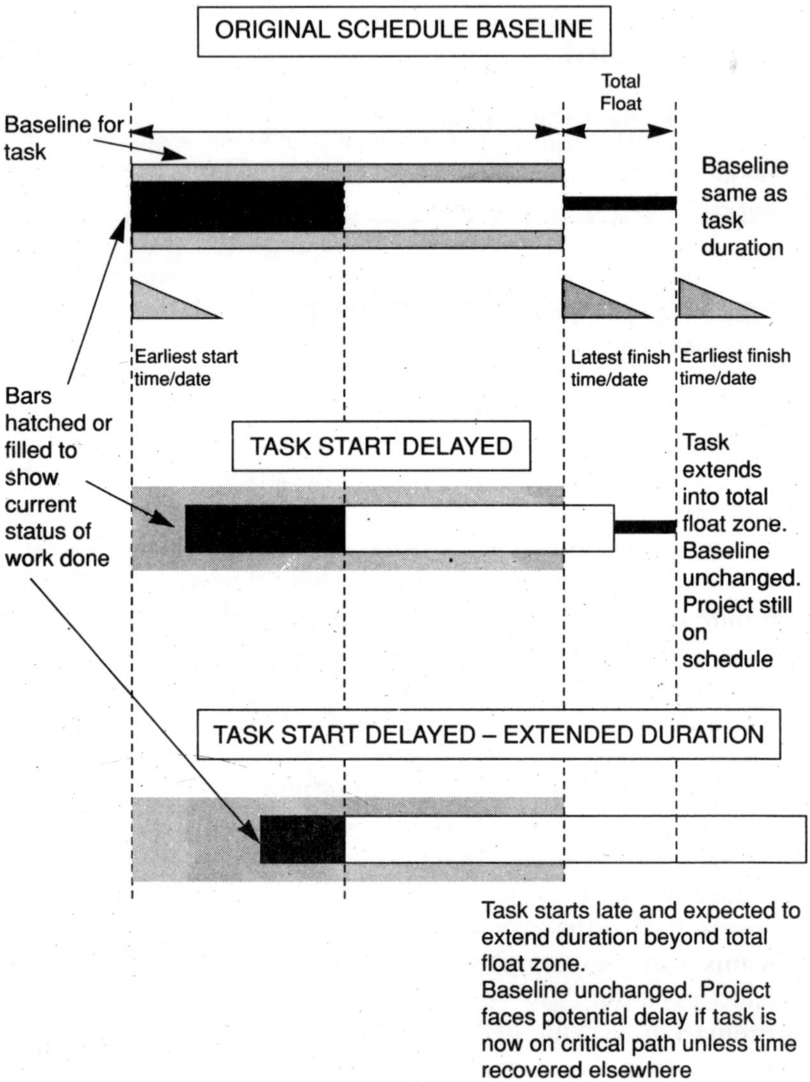

Figure 9.5 *Showing progress on the Gantt chart*

the extended completion date. Serious slippage of non-critical activities may turn them critical, leading to a new critical path for the project. The critical path is never fixed unless everything happens exactly as scheduled.

define completion

Clearly define what everyone understands by completion. The bar on a schedule is a linear graphical representation of effort. In real life, effort is never linear and depends on:

- the accuracy of the detailed planning of tasks to do;
- the complexity of the work;
- the amount of interruptions to the work;
- the availability of data and equipment;
- how the individual feels on the day.

Per cent complete assessments are often quoted in progress reports. These are of little value and you need to know whether the task will finish on time, so ask for a forecast of when it will be completed. This focuses the individual responsible for the work to review other commitments due in the same period and give a more realistic assessment of the time to complete. If the forecast completion date is then clearly unacceptable, take some prompt corrective action. Persuade all your KSOs to get into the habit of forecasting performance for their key stages.

Ensure the progress reports give reasons for any changes to previous forecast completion dates. Encourage the team to develop expertise in accurate forecasting to expose potential future variances. The analysis for variances at all stages must be a primary concern for the whole team, making sure effective corrective action is taken when any issues occur.

Analysis of a variance is essential to expose the causes of the problem. Your primary concern is to maintain schedule integrity – no slippages. Taking corrective action usually has limited possibilities:

- rearrange workload(s) if a milestone date is going to be missed;
- put more effort into the job;
- put additional resources on to the job;
- move the milestone date;
- lower the scope and/or quality of the results demanded by the plan.

Corrective action is normally approached using these options in this order, remembering all could have a cost implication. Record any assumptions you make when deciding action plans – they could have significance later! Before deciding action plans check if:

- the critical path has changed;
- any individual workloads are adversely affected;
- any other milestones are subject to slippage;
- any new HIGH risks are exposed;
- any new ISSUES are exposed;
- any cost over-runs are introduced – do these need approval?
- any localised schedule slippages are controllable.

progress reporting

Check with your customer and the project sponsor that they are getting all the essential information they need. Avoid creating an enormous paper trail. Keep reports short using templates, but expect to make a more detailed presentation occasionally at a full project review. Focus the reports on the project milestones:

- short summary of progress;
- milestones due and completed;
- milestones due that have slipped;
- corrective actions put in place to recover the slippage;
- milestones due in next reporting period;

- issues escalated and waiting for decisions;
- new issues escalated to sponsor or PST;
- forecast of project completion date;
- forecast of project cost at completion;
- any significant changes requested and actions proposed/taken;
- reasons for any revision of previous forecasts.

Project control is dependent on good communication and feedback. Keep the process working to avoid confusion and misunderstandings and ensure all your project records are up to date.

progress meetings

Everyone hates meetings but regular progress meetings are an important part of the project control process to review the current status at any time. Take specific actions to make them effective. Everything that has happened before the meeting is ancient history! Remember that time spent in a meeting is time lost to project work, so:

- keep your progress meetings short – maximum one hour;
- keep meetings to the point and focused on exceptions;
- avoid diversions and problem solving;
- start and finish on time;
- maintain good control;
- have the updated key stage Gantt chart available for reference;
- identify the outstanding issues but do not try to solve them in the meeting – set up a separate discussion with the relevant people.

Focus the team to expose:

- what has been completed on time;
- any outstanding exceptions to the work done;

- what actions agreed earlier are incomplete;
- when outstanding action plans will be complete;
- which milestones are completed on time;
- which milestones have slipped;
- whether action plans are in place to correct slippages;
- any risks escalated to issues;
- issues still waiting to be resolved;
- any resource capacity changes forecast;
- what work is to be done in the next period;
- which milestones are due in the next period;
- what problems are anticipated in the next period;
- any risks that could affect the work in the next period;
- any problems anticipated with third party contracts in the next period;
- any team performance problems and issues;
- whether the business case is still valid.

Always have a flip chart in the meeting room and record agreed actions on the sheet as they occur with responsibility and target completion date. In this way there should be no doubt in the team who is responsible for which actions and they do not have to wait for the minutes. Avoid:

- long verbal reports of what has been done;
- problem solving in the meeting – take serious issues off-line;
- long debates – they detract from the purpose and cause deviation;
- negotiations – usually excludes most of those present;
- 'any other business' – the biggest timewaster!

watchpoint

The action list is the most important document to come out of progress meetings and this is the starting point of the next meeting – checking all agreed actions have been completed.

control the costs

The best way to control your project is to focus on cost measurement. To demonstrate success you must not exceed the budget.

Accurate cost control is only effective if *all* costs are measured, including the costs of people working on the project. This means everyone must record their time spent on project work so that this can be costed. Cost rates often include all indirect costs such as rents, heating, lighting, etc for the organisation. If the time data is not collected in a consistent and disciplined way, then you cannot control the costs very accurately. Your monitoring process must, therefore, include accurate measurement of:

- the time spent on each task;
- the resources used on all tasks;
- cost of materials (and wastage) used;
- cost of equipment time used;
- capital expenditure committed;
- revenue expenditure committed.

Normally these measurements are made over a specific period of two or four weeks or by calendar month. Alternatively you must resort to applying cost rates to the planned resource allocations. This assumes that what actually happens is exactly as planned. As we know this is not true, you must adjust the costs for each activity based on actual start and finish dates.

For effective control you need information on:

- the project budget as fixed in the business case;
- the project operating budget, a cumulative total based on the WBS;

- the costs incurred in the current accounting period;
- the costs incurred to date from the start;
- the work scheduled for completion according to the schedule in the current period;
- the total work scheduled for completion to date;
- the work actually completed in the current period;
- the total work actually completed to date.

The work breakdown structure is the essential budget building tool to derive an operating budget. Then measure costs incurred as the work proceeds and compare with this budget.

> **watchpoint**
>
> When reporting project costs clearly identify variances between the operating budget (based on the plan WBS) and the business case budget. Significant variance may become an issue to be resolved.

cost control measures

Four essential measures are used for the control of project costs:

BAC – budget at completion: this is based on the operating budget developed from the WBS for the whole project.

BCWS – budgeted cost of the work scheduled: at any specific time the schedule shows a certain amount of work should be completed. This is presented as a percentage completion of the total work of the project at that time. Then:

$$\%\ Scheduled\ Completion \times BAC = BCWS$$

BCWP – budgeted cost of the work performed: at any specified time the actual work measured as complete is compared with the scheduled amount and the real percentage completion calculated. Then:

$$\%\ Actual\ Completion \times BAC = BCWP$$

The BCWP is the earned value of the work of the work completed.

ACWP – actual cost of work performed: at any specified time the actual cost incurred for the work. The timing of the actual cost measurement coincides with the percentage completion progress measurement so that the actual cost can be compared with earned value (BCWP).

Other terms often used include:

FTC – forecast to complete: a forecast of the cost to be incurred to complete the remaining work. This may be an extrapolation using an analysis model or simply the best estimates of all the costs to complete the project.

CV – cost variance: the difference between the value of the work performed and the actual cost for that work, that is:

$$CV = BCWP - ACWP$$

If the actual cost is above budget the CV becomes negative!

SV – schedule variance: the difference between the value of the work performed and the value of the work that had been scheduled to be performed, at the same measurement point in time, that is:

$$SV = BCWP - BCWS$$

If the work done is behind schedule the SV becomes negative!

The variance measures are often used for trend analysis, because of their sensitivity to changes as the project progresses.

recording cost data

The simplest way is to tabulate all data using a spreadsheet on a computer to calculate and update the data at regular intervals. Alternatively most project management software includes these standard cost control measures. This makes it easier to incorporate any amendments to the budget resulting from major changes to the project. Most spreadsheets and project software include charting features and the data is then used to automatically generate a chart showing the progress of the BCWP, and ACWP against the BCWS as the project progresses. Keeping your own records of costs also ensures it is regularly updated. It provides you with real-time data to compare with financial budget reports issued from other sources.

10

closure and post-project evaluation

Finally you have overcome what sometimes seemed like 'mission impossible' to enter the final phases of your project. Many issues can still occur and you must continue to monitor carefully to ensure a successful outcome. Closure of a project does not happen, you must plan it with care to follow some specific steps.

Ensure your communication processes keep the sponsor and other management involved right up to the sign-off of the completion certificate. The last thing you want is to become infected with a common virus – 'project drift'.

project drift

This occurs when you take the pressure off the control system and allow the customer or any stakeholder to throw in a few add-ons: 'Just before you finish the project, have a look at this modification?' Control of late changes of mind adds significant extra work and considerable costs to the project. This is often when some sleeping stakeholders suddenly wake up and start making a lot of noise!

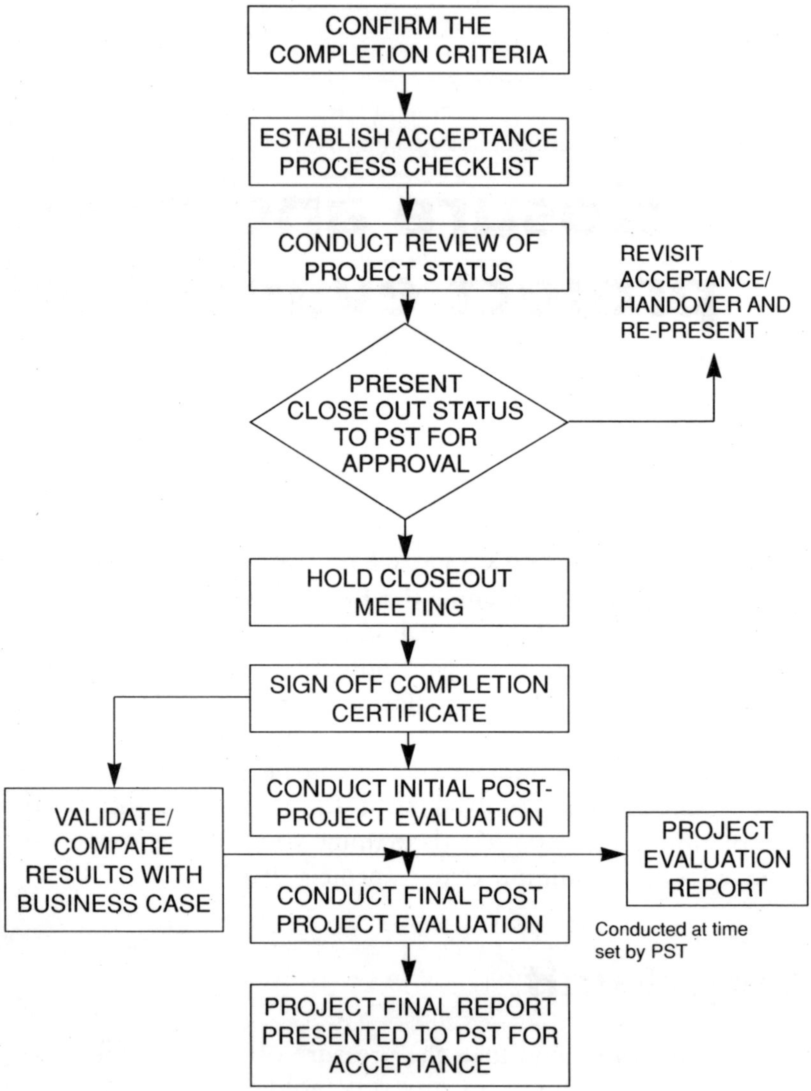

Figure 10.1 *Closure and evaluation process steps*

> **watchpoint**
>
> Late scope changes often cause projects to become 'endless'. Focus everyone on project costs as these always escalate dramatically with project drift.

As closure approaches the team members are concerned about their next assignment and this may show as a reduced motivation with a slowing down of effort and lack of commitment. You must keep the momentum going and avoid losing team members to other projects or operational activities.

set the completion criteria

You should have included the acceptance process in your plan. This will have included just what completion means to your customer and their user group. Check the specific criteria they agreed to use at the outset are still valid. Project completion is signified by:

- all tasks finished;
- agreed deliverables completed;
- testing completed;
- training materials prepared;
- equipment installed and operating;
- documentation manuals finished;
- process procedures finished and tested;
- staff training finished.

All criteria for completion must be measurable by agreed metrics or conflicts will arise.

the acceptance process checklist

For most projects it is easy for the team to identify the essential steps of hand over. Establish a checklist you must agree with your customer and the user group. This checklist includes a list of activities that must be finished before acceptance is confirmed and could include questions about:

- unfinished non-critical work;
- the project tasks done;
- the deliverables achieved;
- quality standards attained;
- supply of equipment;
- installation of equipment;
- testing and validation of equipment;
- testing and validation of operating processes;
- documentation manuals;
- new standard operating procedures;
- design of training programs;
- training of operating staff and management;
- training of maintenance staff;
- setting up a help desk;
- establishing maintenance function;
- outstanding issues awaiting resolution;
- identifying any follow-on projects;
- limits of acceptability;
- who monitors post project performance;
- budget over-runs.

The acceptance process should also identify the customer representative who has the authority to sign the project completion report. In addition confirm:

- who is responsible for each step of the acceptance process and the work involved;

- what post-project support is required and who is responsible;
- what post-project support can be available;
- for how long such support must be given.

Once an agreed process is produced with a hand over checklist you are ready to implement the final stages of the project.

the closeout meeting

Prepare the team well for this important meeting – carry out a full and rigorous review of the project status. Check that all work is finishing on time and no forgotten tasks are still expected. At this stage it is quite common to find a number of outstanding minor tasks from earlier key stages still unfinished. They are not critical and have not impeded progress until now, yet they must be completed.

> **watchpoint**
>
> Agree action plans to complete all forgotten or outstanding tasks to avoid giving your *customer* an excuse to hold up the acceptance.

Focus on outstanding issues and allocate responsibility for each with clear target dates for resolution. When you are satisfied that everything is under control confirm the date of the closeout meeting with your customer and the project sponsor. At this meeting you:

- review the project results achieved;
- go through the handover checklist;
- confirm and explain action plans for any outstanding work to tidy up;

- confirm and explain action plans for any outstanding issues;
- agree and confirm responsibilities for any ongoing work or support;
- confirm who is responsible for monitoring project benefits;
- thank the team and stakeholders for their efforts and support;
- thank the customer and your project sponsor for their support and commitment.

Provided you have done everything the hand over checklist demands, acceptance should be agreed and the completion certificate approved and signed. You can then organise an appropriate celebration for the team and stakeholders!

post-project evaluation

why evaluate?

Evaluation is the process used to review the project and identify: what went well; what went badly; and any variances compared to the business case. Then ask: 'Why?'

what is evaluated?

The technical work, achievements, the project processes and the management of the project are all evaluated. Your success is much more likely to be measured by comparing what is achieved in the weeks or even months after completion with what the business case established.

Evaluation is not to create blame for what did not go well. Evaluation takes place in three modes:

- *active evaluation* – during the project;

- *initial post-project evaluation* – at the point of project closure;
- *final post-project evaluation* – at fixed period after closure.

Each is an important activity and opportunity to learn and confirm that the success sought at the outset has actually been achieved.

active evaluation

An effective project team is always keen to learn from what they are doing. Promote evaluation by encouraging the team to question the way they carry out the project work. This is particularly valid when issues are resolved by asking relevant questions. There are no rules for evaluation, just let the team focus on identifying opportunities for learning. This is continuous improvement in action leading to better ways of doing things. What is more important is that anything learned must be accepted and broadcast so everyone can benefit from the experience.

initial post-project evaluation

Valuable experience and information are gained during a project. Much of this is lost in project archives and never recovered to help future project teams. At the point of closure the lessons learnt during a project should be documented and distributed to individuals engaged or likely to be engaged in project activities. Opportunities for improving processes and procedures are often identified during a project when everyone is too busy to make changes. These opportunities can soon get lost in the mists of time.

It is appropriate to carry out post-project evaluation asking in-depth and searching questions about:

- how the work was carried out;
- the processes and procedures employed;
- how you managed the risks and issues;
- the effectiveness of managing the stakeholders.

Remember the purpose of this whole process is to learn.

An initial technical evaluation is concerned to demonstrate that the best results were obtained with the skills, experience and technology available to you throughout the project. You need to focus the team to identify:

- where successes were achieved;
- where technical problems occurred;
- how creativity and innovation was encouraged during the project.

Much can be learnt from this evaluation which adds to the growth of knowledge in the organisation. Recognise that your technical achievements may have a value to others, often far more than you can realise at the current time. Do ensure that the technical part of your evaluation report is distributed to anyone who could benefit from your efforts. You can similarly learn from the efforts of your colleagues with other projects.

final post-project evaluation

This is focused on two areas of the project performance: a further technical evaluation; and evaluation of business case forecasts. The difficulty here is that several months after completion you may have moved on to another project and someone else is responsible for the ongoing activity of evaluation. However, it is important for the PST to get a report at some agreed time after completion about this ongoing performance. Was the project worth doing after all the effort? It is easy to forget the project and what it cost the organisation if no performance measurement is carried out.

A further technical performance review is valid to check the results are still delighting the customers. A check can ensure the results measure up to forecasts and that no serious ongoing service, reliability or maintenance issues have surfaced.

The project benefits should be measured and compared with the final version of the business case. All the benefits of the project are not immediately apparent. At the definition phase of the project you set out the project benefits. All of these benefits were quantified with agreed metrics to assess performance. The results must be compared with the cost-benefit analysis along with all the other forecast benefits that the project was planned to provide the organisation. This data is important feedback to the PST and their decision-making process. Although as the project manager you have moved on to another project at the closure, you will almost certainly want to get regular reports of performance over the following months. When the benefits accumulate later, give the team members some feedback – they will be interested.

and finally...

You have finished the project, delighted your customer and reported your evaluation in a final report. Now you can celebrate with your team – a job well done! Call a celebration team meeting and ask the customer and other stakeholders to come along. Ask your project sponsor to address the group and put on record the success achieved.

watchpoint

Share success with your team, without whom the outcome may have been quite different. Give recognition to the contribution of everyone involved.

further reading

Barker, A (1993) *Making Meetings Work*, The Industrial Society, London

Carter, B, Hancock, T, Morin, J-M and Robins, N (1996) *Introducing Riskman*, The Stationery Office, Norwich

Davenport, J and Lipton, G (1993) *Communications for Managers*, The Industrial Society, London

Eales-White, R (1992) *The Power of Persuasion*, Kogan Page, London

Frame, J D (1994) *The New Project Management*, Jossey-Bass Inc, San Francisco

Graham, R J and Englund, R L (1997) *Creating an Environment for Successful Projects*, Jossey-Bass Inc, San Francisco

Lockyer, K (1984) *Critical Path Analysis and other Project Network Techniques*, Pitman, London

Pokras, S (1998) *Systematic Problem-Solving and Decision-Making*, 2nd edn, Kogan Page, London

Rosenau, M D (1991) *Successful Project Management*, Van Nostrand Reinhold, New York

Young, T L (1993) *Leading Projects*, The Industrial Society, London

Young, T L (1998) *The Handbook of Project Management*, revised edn, Kogan Page, London